"This book has many ideas about how to really engage business in schools and the education of children because Patricia Alper has masterfully written about a model with clarity, giving solid examples while being engaging. I have no doubt this model would work in the real world of schools and be impactful for both mentors and their mentees. Especially compelling is the description of project based learning which could be used in teacher preparation programs in order to teach students how to implement active learning projects . . . it is particularly insightful about selecting the right project and placing it within the mentors' professional experience. I have rarely seen any proposed relationship between business and education to be so meaningful, building on the strengths of each partner and enhancing the work of both."

—Mari Koerner, PhD, dean of Mary Lou Fulton
Teachers College, Arizona State University

"With clear writing and fascinating case studies, Patricia Alper presents the business world with a compelling call to service. Unlike more general approaches to mentoring, engaging youth in project based learning is intuitive, scalable, and broadly applicable. As the book makes clear, mentoring that is grounded in shared interests and the expertise of mentors represents one of the best hopes for bridging the social capital gap, opening doors, and ultimately enriching the lives of many."

—Dr. Jean Rhodes, Frank L. Boyden Professor
of Psychology, University of Massachusetts, Boston;
director of the Center for Evidence-Based Mentoring

"I have to tell you—your work gave me goosebumps. Not only do I love your writing style, I think it's great that your work is grounded in your personal experience. Most importantly, your message reflects the core tenets of our organization's mission, and coincides with my own professional beliefs."

—Rebecca A. Corbin, EdD, president and CEO,
The National Association of Community College
Entrepreneurship (NACCE)

"I had the pleasure of reading excerpts from your book—I love the writing—it's crisp and real. For the corporate sector, the collection of case studies in one single place is going to be so helpful, particularly for those who want to talk about honest-to-goodness commitment and engagement. Thank you for taking on this project."

—Deborah Holmes, Americas director, corporate social responsibility, Ernst & Young LLP

"Patty makes a compelling case that if we're serious about closing the opportunity gap in school and work, we need more caring adults to get involved as mentors. We need a mentoring revolution. *Teach to Work* is a passionate, firsthand account of how to mentor well from someone who has been serving on the front lines. This is an invaluable resource for individual volunteers, corporate community relations teams, and school partners."

—Nick Hutchinson, executive director, US2020

"Leveraging the unique skill sets of our employees and allowing them to bring their 'whole self' to a volunteer experience has proven to be a win–win for all. Employees are proactively seeking mentoring opportunities while mentees are benefiting from our community outreach. Patty is spot on that providing a Project Based Mentoring experience is the way to go."

—Susan Warner, vice president, worldwide communications, MasterCard

"In my heart of hearts, Patty, I know you are right when you talk about a Project Based Mentoring experience as the catalyst in an intergenerational mentor–mentee relationship. This idea contributes to the work we have all been doing in mentorship, and I applaud you for taking this on."

—Marc Freedman, founder and CEO of Encore.org, author of *Encore: Finding Work that Matters in the Second Half of Life* and *The Kindness of Strangers*

"Patty, did you ever know 10 years ago, that you could change people's lives? I talk about spiritual genetics in my latest book, where each of us can choose the spirit of who we want to become. It does not have to be within a family's bloodlines. You have made a difference in the lives of these kids, and most likely you have made a difference in the lives of their kids as well. They have grabbed hold of your light, because they feel your encouragement and kindness, and maybe because they had no other. Thank you for your important leadership in this role."

—Chris Gardner, author of *The Pursuit of Happyness*, from his 2010 NFTE "Dare to Dream" speech

TEACH
TO
WORK

TEACH
TO
WORK

How a Mentor, a Mentee, and a Project
Can Close the Skills Gap in America

PATTY ALPER

bibliomotion
inc.

First edition published in 2017
by Bibliomotion, Inc.
711 Third Avenue New York, NY 10017, USA
2 Park Square, Milton Park, Abingdon, Oxon OX14 4RN, UK

© 2017 by Taylor & Francis Group, LLC

Bibliomotion is an imprint of Taylor & Francis Group, an Informa business

No claim to original U.S. Government works

Printed on acid-free paper

International Standard Book Number-13: 978-1-62956-162-2 (Hardback)

Library of Congress Cataloging-in-Publication Data
Names: Alper, Patricia, author.
Title: Teach to work : how a mentor, a mentee, and a project can close the skills gap in America /
    Patricia Alper.
Description: New York : Bibliomotion, 2017.
Identifiers: LCCN 2016043491 | ISBN 9781629561622 (hardback) | ISBN 9781315211619 (ebook)
Subjects: LCSH: Mentoring—United States. | Ability—United States. | BISAC: BUSINESS &
    ECONOMICS / Education. | BUSINESS & ECONOMICS / Training.
Classification: LCC BF637.M45 A47 2017 | DDC 658.3/124—dc23
LC record available at https://lccn.loc.gov/2016043491

Visit the Taylor & Francis Web site at
http://www.taylorandfrancis.com

All Trademark Applications are submitted by
The Alper Portfolio Group to include:
Teach to Work™
Teach2Work™
Project Based Mentoring™

Note 1: This book is written based on *many of my own personal* experiences of mentoring day to day and helping create the Adopt a Class model with the Network for Teaching Entrepreneurship (NFTE). Going forward, Adopt a Class remains a wonderful and meaningful engagement which I continue to be a part of; that said, time and leadership have modified elements of the current NFTE volunteer model. This book does *not* represent NFTE's current views or practices.

Note 2: All student letters included in this book are written verbatim from correspondence submitted to the author. Only first names have been used and/or changed to protect student privacy.

Printed and bound in the United States of America by Sheridan

COME TO THE EDGE,
SHE SAID.
THEY SAID, WE ARE
AFRAID.
COME TO THE EDGE,
SHE SAID.
THEY CAME.
SHE PUSHED THEM . . .
AND THEY FLEW!!!!!!!

SEKEITHIA, 2006 MENTEE / RECORDED POET

I am dedicating this book to the Network for Teaching Entrepreneurship (NFTE), without which I would never have had the life-changing experience of working shoulder to shoulder directly with youth, developed the drive to innovate a pilot volunteer model that is based on a deep student–mentor relationship with recurring visits, or have found a creative pathway that connects all disciplines in business with the education sector.

I wish to commemorate:

- my dear NFTE family of associates, with whom I have worked for all these years, including the wonderful six-hundred-plus students I've had the great privilege of mentoring;
- my co-mentor, who has been visiting classrooms with me for more than fifteen years and helped shape this concept;
- the teachers who welcomed us into their classrooms, first as interlopers and then as partners in education;
- the Washington, D.C., staff and board, who, as a team, stood behind this mentorship program with enthusiasm, participation, and belief;
- all the NFTE mentors nationally who have taken on this calling and who remain my heroes;
- my fellow national board members, executive team, and headquarters staff, who are the visionaries for global entrepreneurship education; and
- the founder, who had the brilliance to dream, write, and execute NFTE, which has changed the lives of youth worldwide.

With this dedication, I would also like to pledge a percentage of royalties to the NFTE organization, where the funds will continue to support and grow NFTE's mentoring programs.

Patty

Contents

FOREWORD

Imagine if a country created a true human development pipeline for all individuals—one that starts at birth and doesn't stop until death. This image brings new meaning to how we might think about our educational system and our broader employer ecosystem—because it would mean building seamless linkages between early childhood learning; primary, secondary, and tertiary education; and employers of all shapes and sizes. We have nothing close to this vision of a human development pipeline today. In fact, it's easier to argue that our educational system—and its links to emplo–yers—is utterly broken. They are more like castles with large moats between them than a seamlessly integrated human development pipeline.

We can influence this trajectory of human development, which passes through educational systems and leads toward having great jobs (being engaged at work) and great lives (thriving in well-being). All of us, either individually or at an organizational level, can "do" something to improve this. And that is why Patty Alper's book becomes so important. It defines an active role for the business sector through mentorship of students.

Here is one powerful example of why this is needed and where the pipeline breaks down.

In recent Gallup studies, we learned that 98 percent of chief academic officers at colleges and universities say they are confident they are preparing students for success in the workplace. Yet only 13 percent of U.S. adults strongly agree that college graduates are well prepared for success in the workplace, and only 11 percent of C-level business executives strongly agree college graduates have the skills they are looking for. Whether perception, reality, or a combination of the two, this is a huge gap in our understanding of work readiness for college graduates.

Gallup has done decades of research—all over the world—studying what it means to have a great job and a great life. For the past two years, Gallup (in partnership with Purdue University and the Lumina Foundation) has conducted the largest representative study of college graduates in U.S. history—annually collecting responses from thirty thousand college graduates. We have studied their long-term outcomes toward achieving great jobs and great lives—measuring not just their levels of employment and their household and personal income, but also the degree to which they are engaged in their work and thriving in their overall well-being. What we have learned has begun to change the conversation in higher education about what matters most in a student's experience *during* college that relates to work and life success *after* college.

Gallup identified six key factors that, when experienced by graduates during college, doubled their odds of being engaged in their work and having a greater sense of well-being later in life. Ask yourself these questions and answer on a scale of 1–5, with 5 being that you "strongly agree":

- I had at least one professor who made me excited about learning.
- The professors at my alma mater cared about me as a person.
- I had a mentor who encouraged my goals and dreams.
- I worked on a long-term project that took a semester or more to complete.
- I had a job or internship where I applied what I was learning in the classroom.
- I was extremely involved in an extracurricular activity or organization.

If you strongly agree with any of these six statements, your experience likely had a profound effect on how engaged you are in your work and whether you are thriving in your life. And this is why Patty Alper's book and work are so important. Her entire model focuses on deep mentoring for students and applying what they are learning through long-term projects based on real-world experience. In short, it's a model that perfectly reflects Gallup's important findings on this subject. College graduates who had mentors encouraging their goals and dreams, internships, or long term projects where they applied what they were learning, double their odds of achieving a great job and a great life compared with their peers who did not. Great news if you hit these marks! And had an encouraging pathway to successful outcomes!

The dilemma is that few college graduates hit the mark on these critical experiences and support. A mere 22 percent of all college graduates in the U.S. strongly agree that they had a mentor who encouraged their goals and dreams. Only 32 percent strongly agree that they had a job or internship where they applied what they were learning.

The problem that Patty Alper outlines in this book is scaling these critical experiences for all students. The opportunity she has seized upon is as compelling as any. Her model of combining the potent ingredients of mentoring and real-world project based learning is a formula for success. We can only hope that educational institutions and employers of all shapes and sizes race to support this kind of work everywhere. I know of no better way of building young people's ideas and energy for the future than through mentors who encourage their goals and dreams and through real experiences that connect the dots between their learning and the real world.

Brandon H. Busteed
Executive Director, Education and Workforce Development
Gallup, Inc.

PREFACE

A Snapshot

A Mentor

In this book you will learn that you, as a mentor with a unique professional background, will be sharing your knowledge and your expertise, as well as your life's experiences, in a meaningful way. You will be working with mentees (students) mostly one on one in a school or after-school setting, supporting the work of a teacher or leader in an adjunct capacity. These contributions, over a semester or full year, will lead you to a fulfilling engagement, a commitment to community, and a special form of giving. You will transform lives one student at a time and teach kids real-world skills while simultaneously enhancing your own.

A Mentee

A mentee will benefit from your attention, learning soft skills, collaboration, problem solving, and oral presentation techniques, all while tackling projects with real impact. By working side by side with you, a knowledgeable practitioner, your mentees will gain new confidence and motivation and you will make learning relevant. You will help them reimagine their futures and better prepare them for the twenty-first-century job market.

A Project

Project Based Mentoring™ is a unique approach to learning. The model stems from Project Based Learning theories, integrating a mentor and mentee, two different generations and culturally diverse people, around something to "do." The project is based on tackling realistic problems with real-world application. While the mentor has vast experience in the project dimensions and content, the student is the idea generator, the responsible party, and the driver of the activity and its execution. Together, the mentor and mentee share a mutual goal for planning the project framework within a timeline to achieve successful completion and a public oral defense. The project and the relationship mimic workplace assignments and intergenerational work relationships.

A School

A school or an educational nonprofit works as a liaison to place mentors in classrooms. The learning institution provides the setting, curriculum structure, "project" assignment, and teacher. The mentor holds an adjunct role and works hand in hand with educators to prepare students for success in life by working with them on real-world issues.

ACKNOWLEDGMENTS

The following people all remain touch points for support, guidance, and inspiration:

Contributing writers: Trish Donnally, Tim Carrington, Sunny Kaplan
Researchers: Leah LaCivita, Connor Smith
Publisher/editorial guidance: Taylor and Francis team: Mike Sinocchi, Jonathan Mack, Gina Almond, and Media Connect associates; Bibliomotion team: Erika Heilman, Jill Friedlander, Susan Lauzau, Alicia Simmons
Advice, introductions: Kate Britton, Dan Delany, Perry Hooks, Sam Horn, Julie Kantor, Caitlin Olson, Shawn Osborne, Steve Mariotti, Barbara McNichol, Elizabeth Rich, Larry Robertson, Amy Rosen, Elizabeth Smith
Co-classroom mentors: Maryland/DC: Phil McNeill, Celie Neihaus; Florida: Stuart Halpert, Rick Smith
Influencers: Marc Brackett, David Brooks, Walter Bumphus, Brandon Busteed, Enrique Celaya, Maureen Conway, Jim Clifton, Carlos Contreros, Michael Crow, Clinton Family, Gene Cohen*, Rebecca Corbin, Carol Dweck, Edie Frasier, Marc Freedman, Tom and Ann Friedman, Howard Gardner, Chris Gardner, Susan Harmeling, Brett Hunt, Nick Hutchinson, Walter Isaacson, Mary Koerner, Jeff Kudisch, Eric Lui, Jodi Lipson, Jamie Mertosis, Adam Meyerson, Dave Nelson, Penny Pritzker, Robert Putnam, Jean Rhodes, Dov Seidman, Eric Schwartz, Howard Schultz, David Shapiro, Shimon Shokek

Friends: Adrienne, Anne, Carmen, Cheryl, Christie, Jane, Jill, Leslie, Linn, Lorraine, Michelle L, Michelle S, Sandi, Shelly, Sue, Sunny, Thew, Tina

Family: David, Carolyn, Richard, Kate, Alex, Mychael, Allison, Mason, Lauren, Rick, Shirley, Albert, Jane, Sonny, Tina, Benjamin, Albert, Susan, Gerald, Steven, Robert, Jimmy, Ana, Isabella, Gabriella, Nancy, Ralph, Scott, Ari, John, Sue, Lucy, David, *Morton, *Lillian, *Albert, *Fanny, *Sol, *Melvin

(*posthumously)

INTRODUCTION

If it weren't for you I wouldn't be where I am today running my own business and loving what I am doing.

—Khaled, a high school student

Mentoring transforms lives. I have learned this firsthand through the eyes of some six hundred inner-city high school students I have had the privilege of mentoring over the last fifteen years. In *Teach to Work,* I will show how you can improve the lives of high school, community college, or university students—while simultaneously enhancing your own.

A breakdown exists between the preparation students receive in America's schools and the skills they need to enter and succeed in the twenty-first-century job market. This is particularly true in low-income communities, where economic conditions can be predictors of failure, and where a vicious cycle is often fed by rampant poverty and single-parent households. In these expanding pockets of our society, a deficit of success can easily exist: students rarely meet role models to emulate. This population of youth often reaches adulthood without ever encountering successful, fulfilled adults who inspire the belief: "I could be doing some version of what they are doing."

Students often lack the soft skills usually gleaned from role models. This problem is enhanced by the advent of Internet communication and the way we interact business to business and person to person. As Claire Cain Miller pointed out in her October 2015 *New York Times* article, "Best Jobs Require

Social Skills," to better prepare students for the workforce, traditional schools may need to revisit what they are teaching. In describing today's education, she writes, "To prepare students for change in the way we work, the skills schools teach many need to change. . . . Social skills are rarely emphasized."[1]

Tim Kautz and James J. Heckman, a Nobel Prize–winning economist, did research on what they call non-cognitive skills, such as character, motivation, and goals, which are considered extremely valuable traits in the labor market. Their studies suggest that "character" is a skill, not a trait; that its development is a dynamic process that can be taught; and that non-cognitive skills (social skills) are as important as cognitive skills. Last, they concluded that successful educational interventions should emulate mentoring environments.[2]

The big idea I am proposing in this book is that we close the chasm between the worlds of business and education. America is abundantly rich in adults with know-how. By connecting mentors—educated adults with expertise and knowledge to share—and mentees—teens and young adults who lack motivation, experience, or successful role models in their lives—we can begin to close the skills gap dramatically. As I see it, we can prepare the next generation for the jobs of tomorrow by adding *real-world, project based experience* to their education.

Imagine building a corps of mentors who give back expertise—both hard and soft skills—to America's youth. This book offers guidance on being a mentor with an easy to follow, step-by-step path that incorporates Why, How, and Where you can mentor.

My idea for *Teach to Work* began to develop when I was a board member for the Network for Teaching Entrepreneurship (NFTE, pronounced "nifty"). I believed so deeply in this mentorship concept that I stepped off the board, wrote a consulting proposal, and for two and a half years, part time, developed and ran a program called Adopt-a-Class. I introduced business mentors to NFTE's entrepreneur students in my hometown of Washington, D.C. Between 2001 and 2014 (the most recent tabulation) the Adopt-a-Class program grew to eleven cities across the United States from the corporate, business, or retired sectors. Today, as NFTE scales its growth, there are many levels of volunteerism, be it for an hour or a day, to guest speak, or to judge a business plan. However, this book highlights a more in-depth mentor-mentee experience with recurring visits. *Teach to Work* expands upon this entrepreneurship model to include all fields: why can't—bankers, lawyers, scientists, engineers, computer specialists, accountants, artists, and others—take on mentoring roles as well?

In *Teach to Work*, we have created a framework for bringing an organization or a person like you, interested in mentorship, to a classroom of approximately twenty-five to thirty students in a high school, community college, or university, or even in an after-school program. You, with the leadership of your classroom teacher, would challenge each mentee to design her own project, develop a master plan to execute it, and focus on a *real-world* problem or need, hence the new term *Project Based Mentoring* (see chapter 4). You would commit to recurring visits to coach and monitor progress throughout a semester or full school year (based on your schedule). You would meet students one on one and provide skill-based coaching, strategic oversight, logistical suggestions, and guidance when it comes time to give a formal project presentation.

The most fulfilling part of the experience, and what keeps me coming back year after year, is the reaction I receive from the students. I believe there's no higher value than sharing your knowledge and touching a young person's life. Imagine helping a teen apply his *own* new concept to a real-world problem, learn marketable skills, and develop the confidence to pursue future opportunities. That is my raison d'etre for writing *Teach to Work*. When students I have mentored come back ten years later and share their continued successes—graduations, new ventures, life passages—I fully realize and embrace the importance of this work. You can too!

I am but one business-minded individual who has experienced great joy and creativity in my role as a mentor. I have received rich rewards, built friendships, and enjoyed successes through this experience. The thousands of letters I have received over the years from students have genuinely touched my heart. Indeed, they have motivated me to explain and promote this concept far and wide.

Consider one student, Khaled, who came from Egypt and started class four months late. On a December day, in Arlington, Virginia, he entered a NFTE entrepreneurship class, though he had little interest in business.

Only fourteen, the youngest freshman in a class of thirty upperclassmen, the then-shy young man clearly lacked confidence. I remember the first day Khaled was there, a new face in the back of the classroom. At the time, my co-mentor, venture capitalist Phil McNeill, and I were eliciting business ideas from all the students, following our own introductions.

I was sharing my experience of developing my commercial construction company. I often like to backtrack and describe my struggle of starting as a "lost" high school student, not loving studying or ever getting great grades. It wasn't until later that I lucked into business. My husband pleaded with me to use my marketing expertise to help him launch an interior project management / construction company, a challenge that was pivotal in my growth. I loved building something from nothing. I shared with the students that it was the first time I had ever used "all" my resources—my blood, sweat, and tears. I learned to absolutely love business—the risk, signing on the dotted line, the strategic thinking, learning the competition, differentiation, winning new clients, and making a profit. I relished our growth, from three to a hundred management-level employees in four years. Oh, how I wished I had learned about business when I was in high school—"This is an opportunity you should not pass up!" I proclaimed.

As I was sharing my story, I had no idea, of course, of the full impact it would have on Khaled or any other student. That is, until I received this letter at the end of the school year:

Miss Patty, I remember the first day I was in class and you were asking everyone to describe their business. I was the only one who didn't have one, and I really didn't care. At that time, business was not one of my goals, but the way you talked about it and gave everyone advice, because of that I decided to accept the challenge . . . If it weren't for you I wouldn't be where I am today running my own business and loving what I am doing.

Khaled overcame his obstacles in full glory. Between his NFTE teacher, Maureen Naughton, an outstanding entrepreneurship curriculum, and dedicated mentors, his business creation, Delicious New York Honey-Made Cookies, got traction. Serious traction! His motivation was to make delicious cookies that were also healthy. He substituted honey in place of sugar to reduce the calories. His five-inch round cookies were only 106 calories each, and were truly delicious, I might add. After months of one-on-one coaching coupled with his diligent, go-for-it spirit, Khaled won the in-class business plan competition, with its prize of $150. He went on to win the regional competition and an award of $1,500, and ultimately finished fifth in the national competition, winning $3,000. Khaled worked arduously and con-quered his fear of public speaking as he slayed the judges with his knowledge, detailed answers, and tasty treats. His new niche: cookies that helped battle overweight inclinations by offering a healthier, lower-calorie alternative.

By the time Khaled was sixteen, he had negotiated with Harris Teeter to use its commercial kitchens and sell his cookies—and had landed Target and Giant Foods as outlets. In those two years, Khaled sold close to thirty-two thousand cookies with a gross mark up of 75 percent.

In *Teach to Work*, you will discover many success stories similar to Khaled's that illustrate these underlying principles and the value-add of having adjunct mentors work with students. This comprehensive guide is written for the potential mentor who has so much to offer but feels reticent, wondering, "How would I work with kids?" Various chapters address meeting the teacher, overcoming first-day jitters, building one-on-one rapport with students, and maintaining motivation—also included are easy-to-follow lesson plans. You will learn how a Project Based Mentoring experience provides tremendous opportunities for corporations, mentors, students, and teachers, and you will see how each mentee develops and presents a proposed plan to a panel of judges, which helps the student build self-confidence and reimagine her future. You will discover that, inevitably, an awakening occurs from this experi-ence. You will explore how creativity can flourish when a mentor truly engages a mentee, how ideas begin to flow, and how students begin to aim high.

Finally, in "A Call to Action" at the end of the book, you will find a national mentoring guide to scores of nonprofit and educational establishments across the country, where mentors can seize the opportunity to share their knowledge based on their own expertise. The United States is so rich in resources that can be channeled toward a Project Based Mentoring experience, whether in school settings or outside. Imagine if these vast pools of skilled mentors could tap into their valuable work knowledge, share it, and transform students' lives.

Consider what could happen if you told your story to a young person who might never have met a successful adult in your area of expertise. Think about what it would be like if your presence and input helped spur growth that led your pupil to innovation or an unimagined path. Unfortunately, you may not recognize your own potential to assume this role, or if you have such an inkling, you are not sure of how to put your desire into action.

I have written *Teach to Work* to provide a step-by-step guide, based on my own fifteen years of mentoring experience, that will help you learn how to connect with youth, potentially find a not-for-profit organization or school to engage with, unleash your mentee's potential, and ultimately help close the skills gap in America. I will show you *why*, *how*, and *where* mentors can mentor. I want to motivate thousands—no, millions—to share their know-how with high school, community college, and university students, or even to launch student-mentored projects on their own. I hope this book will be used as collateral training information for mentors from a peer-to-peer perspective and possibly inspire ideas for creating innovative student projects through a Project Based Mentoring formula. I want to launch the ideas in *Teach to Work* across America and share the valuable lessons I have learned. I know this concept works and will show you how to implement it in the following pages. Join me on this journey and learn how you, too, can transform lives, one student at a time.

Notes

1. Claire Cain Miller, "The Best Jobs Require Social Skills," *New York Times*, October 18, 2015.
2. James Heckman and Tim Kautz, "Fostering and Measuring Skills: Interventions That Improve Character and Cognition," Working Paper 19656, National Bureau of Economic Research, Cambridge, MA, 2013.

PART ONE

Why Mentor

CHAPTER 1

GIVING CORPORATIONS A SOUL

The Benefits of a Workforce
That Mentors

Employees want to be part of something that is bigger than a company. The business culture is internally based, but the philanthropy is external. That volunteer ethos provides something more than a quarterly return on earnings . . . it stretches employees beyond their day-to-day job.
—Rick Luftglass, former director of The Pfizer
Foundation's education volunteer programs

In my professional years of building companies, consulting with companies, working for companies, and, now, striving to understand companies' philanthropic logic and motivations, I have asked myself: What is the intrinsic reward for giving back to a community? Why would a private company get involved with a volunteer mentorship program like the one outlined in *Teach to Work*, operating in local high schools, community colleges, or universities? And, can a private company that mentors students help these kids overcome their lack of clear goals, marketable skills, and aspirations to succeed?

As we tell teen and young adult students—who may never have met anyone who runs an enterprise—a company is a complex organism whose success is determined by management decisions and investments, as well as by a host of external factors that influence the perceptions and behavior of customers, shareholders, employees, competitors, and suppliers. A healthy company doing business in an unhealthy environment won't stay healthy for long. Businesses affect and are affected by the physical and social environments in which they operate. When businesses mislead shareholders or pollute the environment because they are cutting corners, they intensify a climate of distrust.

Conversely, when a company invests in people, deals transparently with the public, and takes responsibility for its environmental footprint, it almost certainly enhances levels of trust. When companies reach beyond their immediate, narrowly defined interests and in some way address larger societal challenges, they pay it forward, generating goodwill and greater trust in the communities they touch.

The Generations to Come

In creating the framework featured in *Teach to Work*, and in working with mentoring programs during the fifteen years leading up to its creation, I became interested chiefly in the generations to come. That is, I started to think more about the next generation of workers and consumers. Who will make up the workforce, and how and where will these employees acquire their skills? What will motivate them? How will they define success? As increasingly complex challenges emerge in a resource-hungry world of seven billion-plus people: Is the next generation of workers likely to be part of the solution or part of the threat?

These questions bring me face to face with what many consider the core challenge for our society—equipping America's young people with the skills they will need to contribute and succeed in a fast-changing, interconnected global economy. They will need to think critically, to innovate, to make midcourse corrections, and to collaborate.

Three thousand senior business executives from twenty-five countries were interviewed for General Electric's 2013 *Global Innovation Barometer*. An alarming four out of five identified their top concern as *a need to better align the education system with business needs*. But here is the biggest concern: just 55 percent of the executives interviewed saw universities and schools as providing a strong model for tomorrow's innovative leaders.

Therefore, education—meaning both skills and a highly developed capacity to apply them—is one of those factors outside the company building that is going to influence how well firms do in the future. So why should a private company get involved in mentoring students? The first big reason is to serve the company's own long-term interests by adding to the pool of employable young people who possess the skills and attitudes that will make them a productive part of the workforce.

No Company Is an Island

Taking another step back, it's important to remember that companies aren't isolated profit machines. They may have corporate structures and corporate cultures that play important roles in their successes, but companies don't and can't operate in a vacuum. They are players within a larger whole—whether a society, a community, a political economy, or a group of people whose attitudes, understandings, and behaviors influence how well the company will perform. Out of this understanding came the corporate social responsibility (CSR) movement.

A few of the early CSR programs in the 1970s were cynically conceived public-relations efforts that were perceived as charitable diversions, while the companies operated in ways that subtracted more from the public good than their token contributions could ever offset. As they trickled out a few donations while sustaining exploitive labor practices or sloppy environmental controls, these practices usually increased a general sense of mistrust for the company.

In a 2006 *Harvard Business Review* article, "Strategy and Society: The Link Between Competitive Advantage and Corporate Social Responsibility," Michael Porter and Mark R. Kramer, global experts on competitiveness, urged companies to steer clear of disconnected charity work and to link CSR activities to strategic competitive goals. The authors praised Microsoft for its partnership with the American Association of Community Colleges (AACC), an effort to address shortages of information technology workers.

Microsoft's $50 million, five-year initiative included financial and product contributions, along with employee volunteers who visited the schools to assess needs, help with curriculum development, and create faculty development institutes.

Today, companies report that having robust CSR and volunteer programs introduces another dimension to company life, bringing a broader sense of purpose to the different layers of the organization—from entry-level staff to the CEO. Employees report feeling happier and more satisfied with their jobs. Teamwork can improve as a result of volunteer programs, and more fulfilled employees show better job performance. Higher morale, improved employee productivity, and better retention can result.

Paying attention to organizational values may even improve the bottom line, according to a 2008 study titled *Corporate Citizenship: Profiting from a Sustainable Business,* by the Economist Intelligence Unit. "Seventy-four percent of respondents to the survey say corporate citizenship can help increase profits at their company," the study said, specifying that strong CSR can affect revenue growth, increasing both profit and cost savings.[1]

Companies tell their own CSR stories best. What follows are testimonies from Starbucks, Zappos, MasterCard Worldwide, Pfizer, Comcast, Ernst & Young, and 3M. While each corporation approaches CSR differently, the volunteer programs and community involvements seem to strengthen the intangibles that help companies build loyal customers and productive employees.

Based on the variety and scope of philanthropic programs, I am convinced that corporations are an *untapped treasury* that is only just beginning to fill a mentorship gap in American schools. Too many students are left outside of productive work life, and too many employers are searching for qualified workers they can hire and retain. Benefits emerge for mentors, mentees, and corporations, as you will discover from the following case studies. I pose a question at the beginning of each that has broad relevance for all companies and their employees. Consider these and you will find the answers crystallize as you continue to read.

Starbucks: A Company with a Soul

Q. How Can Your Company Show Its Soul?

Howard Schultz, chairman and chief executive officer of Starbucks, is an entrepreneur who stands up for what he believes is right—in part due to his background. Schultz grew up in Brooklyn, New York, in public housing, and when he was seven years old, his family lost its health insurance for about a year and a half. "This scarred me," he said. "We all carry our childhood experiences with us." Schultz said his upbringing breeds an awareness of and empathy for struggling, often discouraged, Americans. His background also influences the way he runs his company.

"There's a new movement not just about making money but about a balance of community responsibility. These rules of engagement are changing public companies. My question is, 'How can we use our scale for good?' Profit cannot be the only goal," Schultz said during an interview with *New York Times* opinion columnist Joe Nocera at the Aspen Institute's 2012 Ideas Festival, where I was in the audience.

Schultz told a story about a large institutional shareholder who advocated reducing the company's employee health-care coverage during the financial crisis in 2008, a time when health care was a $250 million line item for Starbucks. Schultz had been looking at ways to cut costs, but said, "The one cost (cut) I would not entertain was health care for our people." As Schultz explained in his book *Onward,* the institutional investor said, "'Howard, we've owned this stock for a long while. We know you're under tremendous pressure, and we feel very strongly that this is the time to cut the health care benefit.' He went on, 'You've got all the cover and the license in the world. Everyone will understand you had no choice.'"[2]

Schultz recounted the conversation and said he responded, "We would fracture the trust of the entire company if we took that health care benefit away. It's a non-starter." He added, "If you feel as if you can no longer hold the stock as a result of this conversation, then you should sell." Within a week, the stockholder had sold half his shares.

"Your values and guiding principles can't be with you when you only have a tailwind, they have to be with you when you are tested," Schultz said, during the Aspen Institute's 2012 Ideas Festival. Having been part of a family without basic health insurance, he would not allow his employees to be subjected to that same level of insecurity. Even in a down economy, covering this expense was a paramount priority to him.

In another segment of the interview, Schultz said he was concerned about the direction the country is taking. "As I travel around the world—Starbucks is in fifty-eight countries[3]—people are talking to me about 'What happened to America? The world needs America. What happened to the promise of America and the idealism of America?'" Schultz added, "Is this the country that our parents and our grandparents sacrificed so much for?" He later said, "We are on a collision course in which something is going to change. How it's going to change, who's going to change it, when it's going to change, I think it's up to us." Since this interview, Starbucks has built initiatives to try and address issues facing Americans and its employees (partners), like veteran hiring, college tuition, and hiring "opportunity youth."

"I do not believe any company in America can build a sustainable, enduring enterprise by just embracing profitability," Schultz said. "Employees today want to work for a company that they trust. They want to be part of something larger than themselves. And they want to go home at night and share with their friends and family that they are proud of what the company stands for."

During the interview an audience member, a CEO from San Francisco, stood and told a story about his frustrating search for a vice president of sales. He finally found a superstar after three attempts. He said the sole reason his company had come to that candidate's attention was that she had noticed that the firm had made a modest donation to the Down Syndrome Foundation on its CSR page on the website. "She called me and said, 'I work for a *soulless* company . . . Can I come work for a company that does this?'" he recalled. "The benefits of these activities for the people you serve and for your employees far outweigh any kind of costs. There's a groundswell of support or desire for people trying to get that meaning into their lives."

Schultz responded, "I couldn't have said it any better."

Zappos: Creating a Culture of Happiness

Q. What Are Your Company's Values, and How Are These Made Visible in the External World?

"Don't we all do our best work when we're happy?" Susan Waldman wrote in the *Washington Post,* when she interviewed Robert Richman, author of *The Culture Blueprint* and former cultural strategist for America's largest online shoe retailer, Zappos—the Happiness Company (rated number one in customer service by American Express in 2011 and rated number six on the list of "100 Best Companies to Work For" by *Fortune* magazine in 2011[4]). "Aren't we happiest when we feel appreciated, connected with others, and have the chance to contribute to something outside ourselves?" Waldman continued.[5]

In his book, *The Culture Blueprint,* Richman mentions that Zappos, Google, and Apple have all shifted from *metrics* as the key focus—to *values:*[6] But how do you create culture? What are some of the difficult leadership questions? In his book, Richman shares his top three questions regarding values:

1. Does leadership live them?
2. Does the company hire and fire by them?
3. Are values used as decision-making criteria?[7]

Sometimes it's easiest to learn about a company by reading its own postings. A position statement on ZapposInsights.com speaks volumes about the company's values. Listed under the heading "Zappos—Higher Purpose":

- The employee page reads, "At Zappos, we have a simple philosophy: Happy employees = Happy customers."
- The world page reads, "Every once in a while, Zappos likes to get out and about to perform random acts of happiness for the general public."

- The community page reads, "Community integration was one of the driving forces behind the relocation of the Zappos campus in 2013. Rather than remaining insular, we have not only built a campus that serves as a venue for community gatherings and charity events, but we also actively encourage employees to take part in and give back to the surrounding community."

These overarching thoughts merit discussion in any company. And their answers often lead to action. The Zappos philosophy shows that a corporate culture of happiness and well-being finds ways to fold in outreach programs that express the company's community and philanthropic values.

MasterCard Worldwide: The Whole Self

Q. What Employee Talents Can Your Company Share?

Because giving back is an integral part of MasterCard's culture, finding a way to make a difference isn't difficult. "The most significant change in our philanthropy and volunteer programs in the last few years has been recognizing the value in giving employees opportunities to bring their unique skills—their 'whole self'—to a volunteer experience. It's those opportunities that are the most fulfilling and that yield the greatest results," said Susan Warner, vice president of worldwide communications at MasterCard, during my conversations with her.

While MasterCard has always been a philanthropic organization, the company changed course in 2014 when it launched its global employee volunteer initiative, Girls4Tech. The signature education program is a hands-on, inquiry-based platform that connects the core of MasterCard's business to science, technology, engineering, and math (STEM) principles. It teaches young girls that it takes all kinds of interests and skills to pursue a STEM career.

"Through Girls4Tech, we're engaging employees in the very foundation of our business by having them serve as role models and mentors. It's incredibly rewarding," continued Warner.

The curriculum, which is based on global science and math standards, was developed in conjunction with MasterCard's top engineers and technologists. The objectives of the program are threefold:

- To increase the number of girls interested in pursuing STEM subjects
- To expand employee volunteerism around the world
- To educate and engage employees in MasterCard's business and leverage their knowledge to make a real difference

By tapping into the payments technology expertise of its employees, the company is inspiring girls to build the STEM skills they need to become tomorrow's leaders and future problem solvers. To date, more than five thousand girls in nine countries have participated in the program.

Another way the company is using its employees' unique skills is by working with the Network for Teaching Entrepreneurship (NFTE). Across the U.S., Belgium, China, and Mexico, MasterCard volunteers inspire youth from under-resourced communities to stay in school and help spark the entrepreneurial mindset, preparing the students for successful futures.

In her opinion, Warner says there's been a targeted shift over the last few years that has created a "discernable cultural change across the company." Some outcomes she noted include:

Recruitment. CSR is a big selling point during recruitment. Human resources has found that the younger generation, in particular, cares that a potential employer has a social responsibility arm. At MasterCard, millennials make up 39 percent of the employee base.

Skills and leadership development. Volunteer experience is used as a development track. As managers review employees' performance and the skills they need to improve, they suggest a mentoring role to help employees learn and improve their public speaking, group management, and one-on-one relationship building. When employees feel that their contributions have been valued by students, they bring greater confidence to the tasks they take on at work.

Loyalty. Employees who mentor are more committed to the company that has introduced them to new experiences and allowed them to give back to the community. In fact, 87 percent of MasterCard employees equate job satisfaction with volunteering. This level of loyalty creates staying power and reduces staff turnover.

Self-fulfillment. Employees engaged in mentoring often have a greater sense of fulfillment. Outside the normal workday, employees may be better able to reflect on and appreciate the depth of their knowledge and how far they have come.

MasterCard has made great strides in building a volunteer program that utilizes the "whole self" of employees. By using their skills and serving as mentors and role models, employees around the world are making a difference in lasting, meaningful ways.

Pfizer: A Volunteer Culture Cannot Be Manufactured

Q. How Can Each Department in Your Company—Research, Development, Manufacturing, Human Resources, Sales, Marketing, Finance, and Management—Provide Support to Students?

Pfizer, the pharmaceutical company, has a long history of fostering a volunteer culture within the organization. Beginning in the 1940s, ad hoc company volunteers stepped up within their own communities to assist schools with science studies and other educational programs. These activities had profound effects among employees, and today Pfizer is one of the biggest philanthropic givers in the United States.

In the 1980s, former Pfizer chairperson Ed Pratt requested that greater strategic importance be placed on science literacy and American competitiveness. He made it clear this would require more than just a dollar investment mandated from the executive suite. The effort grew over time. By

1993, Pfizer was giving away $9 million annually and had volunteer-driven education programs. At two of Pfizer's research and development sites (in Groton, Connecticut, and Sandwich, England), Pfizer was the largest company in town. Pfizer employees at these locations began volunteering in the local schools, and a shift in attitude toward the corporation began to take shape. This involvement put a new face on the "big corporation" because Pfizer scientists had begun working hand in hand with local students. When Pfizer sales reps called on pharmacists and doctors in town, the families these people were serving had benefited from Pfizer firsthand through their work in the schools. The volunteer program provided a link, a feeling that they were all part of the same community. Volunteering built a common ground.

In 2008, fifteen years later, there were active volunteer programs in nearly twenty locations and the company's contribution budget was a whopping $98 million annually, one of the largest in the United States.

Pfizer employees worked in schools under both short- and long-term arrangements:

> **Short term.** Employees worked alongside students and teachers, helping students with projects, guest lecturing, or assisting with science fair preparations or other presentations.
>
> **Long term.** Employees worked in classrooms over the course of the full academic year, sharing expertise in science and other fields and assisting in building curriculum and capacity with teachers. The departments that were involved and the skills they fostered included:

- *Research and development*: science education
- *Manufacturing*: logistics, engineering timetables/projections, and organizational skills
- *Human resources*: conduct and professionalism
- *Sales*: marketing and presentation skills
- *Headquarters and finance*: financial projections and math applications

The benefits to the company have been vast, and include:

- **Engagement with the community.** Community involvement helps build science and math skills in the communities Pfizer serves, establishing a future employee base.
- **Goodwill.** Legislators notice the good works in the community.
- **Community building.** Working in schools where Pfizer is based puts a face on the company, and often builds common ground between Pfizer employees and other local families, who benefit from the knowledge sharing.
- **Connection.** Volunteering builds connections and team spirit among employees.

When I asked Rick Luftglass, former director of The Pfizer Foundation's education volunteer programs, how the program had impacted employees, he shared his favorite story: "One Pfizer senior scientist who had been with the company for twenty years loved the company, worked hard, but had not left his mark in the sense that he was never part of creating a 'blockbuster' drug or a medical breakthrough." Through his work with the students, however, the scientist regularly saw lightbulbs go off in their heads, and those results were payback for his years of scientific effort.

"It's tangible, there is a sense of accomplishment," said Luftglass. But he added, "A company cannot manufacture that special feeling. It has to come from the experience and sincerity that goes with effort." In the last decade, Pfizer has continued to provide skill-based volunteer and mentoring programs. It has expanded and modified this model as it continues to grow in the time since Luftglass's departure.

Comcast: A Partnership Story

Q. How Can Your Company Creatively Partner with a Nonprofit in Your Community?

When Fred Maahs joined Comcast in 2007 as the new senior director of national partnerships for community investment—he is currently vice president of the Comcast Foundation—he didn't realize that an exciting evolution of Comcast's partnership with Big Brothers Big Sisters of America was on the horizon, and that he would become passionately involved in it. Historically, Comcast had always enjoyed community partnerships with many nonprofits. Then, in early 2008, in a meeting spearheaded by John Alchin, the former co-CFO who was active on the board of Big Brother Big Sisters of Southeastern Pennsylvania, a change began, which ultimately led to the creation of the nation's largest workplace mentoring program, in partnership with BBBS.

The goal was to think outside the box, with the objective of better serving students in one of the most poverty-stricken areas of Philadelphia. The outcome was a program called Beyond School Walls, an innovative workplace-based mentorship program created in partnership with BBBS. Beyond School Walls matches at-risk youth with Comcast employees as part of the company's mission to strengthen individuals and communities through one-to-one mentoring. Today, at Comcast offices in sixteen cities nationwide, a collective of 325 Comcast employees volunteer as "Bigs," meeting twice a month during the school year with student "Littles" (ages six through eighteen) from local schools. It has become such a popular volunteer program that there is a waiting list for employees who want to participate as "Bigs."

"Beyond School Walls works because our employees are passionate about making a difference and being a positive role model for children in the community," said Maahs. "Big Brothers Big Sisters is an outstanding partner and it's amazing to see the Littles' eyes light up when they walk into Comcast and are inspired to think about their own life and career goals and everything they can accomplish."

BBBS interviews the students, determines the matches, trains the Comcast mentors, arranges transportation, and supports the process. When Beyond School Walls is in session, the Comcast facility magically transforms. Typically, a Comcast employee, who may work at any level of the organization, is paired with a student, and that relationship may last for the entire time the student is in the program—and sometimes beyond. Some days, after a twenty-minute lunch together, the mentor pairs listen together to a guest speaker or do an activity, such as a digital literacy training program on a computer.

Maahs gets particularly excited about Reverse Day, when the Comcast Bigs visit their Littles at their school and see the students on their own turf, meet their teachers, and see their classrooms and projects. Maahs said this experience creates a deeper bond for all participants.

As a result of the program, Comcast has won numerous awards, including BBBS's national President's Award, Corporate Mentor of the Year from Mentor.org, and Civic 50 from Bloomberg/Points of Light. Through this partnership, Comcast has provided BBBS with more than $65 million in cash and in-kind support since 2008.

One year after being enrolled in the program, Littles showed significant gains in educational experience and social acceptance, with 85 percent maintaining or improving outcomes related to educational expectations, according to the 2013 BBBS *Youth Outcomes Survey.* Maahs said the data shows that mentees have better grades, are less prone to skipping school, and are more likely to graduate.

One of Comcast's current engineers, Michael Mascaro, was a former Little himself. "It's quite something to come full circle and give this employee a chance to pay it forward with this program," Maahs said.

Takeaways from the Comcast–BBBS partnership include:

- Think outside the box with your nonprofit partner.
- Be clear about your organization's capacity.
- Bring community partners to the facility; in this way, Comcast promotes curiosity and engagement on behalf of other employees and creates demand for mentoring.

Ernst & Young: Baking Volunteerism into the Culture

Q. How Do You Recognize Your Employees in Their Community Efforts, and How Do You Think This Can Benefit Your Company?

"EY's purpose is to 'Build a better working world,' because we believe that business can be a force for good in society," says Deborah K. Holmes,

Americas director of corporate responsibility for Ernst & Young since 2003. "Corporate responsibility adds the greatest value when we foster a culture of skills-based volunteerism, taking the same distinctive services and competencies we use in our business every day and applying them to help solve our communities' most pressing challenges."

EY's signature volunteer program, College MAP, is dedicated to supporting education and developing future generations of talent. Launched in 2009, it is a multiyear group-mentoring program focused on empowering students in underserved high schools to prepare for college and succeed in higher education. The program matches EY mentors (from all levels, backgrounds, and service lines) with groups of local high school students. The group-mentoring model has two advantages: multiple mentors provide insight and guidance to the students in the program, and the student participants become their own supportive academic community.

During monthly workshops, mentors and students explore various topics that aim to develop:

- Awareness, exposing students to different college opportunities and the lifelong benefits of higher education
- Financial readiness, by demystifying the process of applying for financial aid and paying for college
- Persistence, by providing personal support and coaching on life skills that encourage students to complete a four-year degree

College MAP has active sites in thirty U.S. cities, and has helped more than eleven hundred students begin their postsecondary journey. EY has pledged to be in thirty-five cities by 2018 as part of a Clinton Global Initiative commitment.

This reflects, in part, EY's CSR strategy and some of the benefits that accrue:

- EY's business strategy is amplified by its support of nonprofit organizations that promote entrepreneurs' education and equity in the workforce.

- Skills-based volunteering is encouraged to maximize societal impact.
- Colleagues who engage with nonprofits become active participants in the communities they serve, and they develop new business pipelines from these connections.
- Colleagues learn to interact in different ways when they participate together on volunteer teams. They see varied dimensions of their coworkers, and their relationships become stronger as a result.
- The volunteer program may pair a partner-level leader with an early-career professional, such as a first-year accountant or administrative assistant. This mixing of ranks creates a positive dynamic by inspiring early-career and junior staff, building internal networks, and providing leadership exposure.
- Exposing employees to new cultures and experiences expands them as individuals and broadens their worlds. It's a great way for them to learn new business skills, which they take back to their home office.
- Employees volunteer in groups, so individuals have more scheduling flexibility and are able to spend quality volunteer time without impacting their professional responsibilities.
- Employee studies show that EY professionals who participate in firm-sponsored volunteer efforts are more engaged with the firm, and those who are College MAP mentors have *significantly* higher engagement, including better interactions with their managers, longer tenure with the firm, and high performance ratings.

To support EY's commitment to providing meaningful volunteer experiences for its people, the firm has embedded a comprehensive network of community engagement leaders (CELs) across its Americas organization. The CELs work closely with community engagement champions (usually a partner in each geographic region) to help employees use volunteerism as a way to develop their professional skills while also building the firm's CSR brand.

"At EY, corporate responsibility is not a peripheral activity: CR is embedded in our culture and business strategy," says Holmes. "Everything we do in the name of CR at EY extends the reach of our core business and adds credibility to our purpose."

3M: Inspiring Young Scientists

Q. How Can Your Company Help a Community Prosper?

A science-based global innovation company, 3M produces items as diverse as office products like Post-it Notes and health-care and highway-safety products. The company attributes its success to 3M employees applying technologies to "real-world customer needs." Many of these same employees use this innovative know-how to benefit the local community and schools, following a goal of using innovation to "improve *every* life."

Each year, fifteen thousand 3M employees serve more than two hundred thousand volunteer hours throughout the United States. When I interviewed Kim Price, then vice president of the 3M Foundation, she said the company is committed to "making the communities prosper where we prosper."

As part of its community involvement, 3M is committed to fostering the next generation of innovators and works to create future scientists by supporting students and educators in the fields of science, technology, engineering, and mathematics (STEM). The company is particularly involved in local schools in St. Paul, Minnesota, home of 3M's headquarters—a decision supported by Inge Thulin, 3M's chief executive officer. Thulin personally requested a focus be made in inner-city schools on the east side of St. Paul when he came on board in 2012.

Some examples of 3M's involvement in schools include the following:

- The 3M Visiting Wizards program brings 3M employees into elementary schools to spark student interest in science through fun experiments.
- 3M STEP (Science Training Encouragement Program) provides 3M lab internships to local students.

- 3M employees help students succeed through e-mentoring, mock interviewing, and science fairs: approximately fifteen hundred local students receive science fair mentoring and judging from 3M employees each year.
- 3M offers engineering camps and hosts student field trips.

Dick Streeper, coordinator for the 3M–St. Paul Public Schools partnership, has been instrumental in matching employees with students. After thirty years with the company as a lab manager, and now as a retiree, Streeper has served thirteen years as coordinator, connecting thousands of 3Mers with students.

Streeper said science innovation companies complain that they cannot find enough potential employees with competencies in the sciences and math. 3M's school involvement can help fill that gap. Streeper says that what keeps him returning year after year is the idea that "If I can be a facilitator to guide students on their pathway, that is worth its weight in gold and that is why I keep doing this." He said 3M's community involvement:

- Demonstrates that 3M cares and is committed to the community where it is based
- Lifts up "employees' souls" through helping others
- Is a great lab for employee leadership development—they learn governance, negotiation, and how to interact effectively with others
- Portrays a positive example of corporate citizenry

Recap

Corporations represent an *untapped treasury* that is only just beginning to fill a mentorship gap in American schools and community colleges. The stories I've featured here underscore that when companies involve their employees in a significant outreach effort they contribute to future generations through happier, more fulfilled, and more loyal employees; through a healthier community that can more easily prosper in the place the company prospers, and can supply tomorrow's workers; and by becoming a multidimensional organism, capable of innovation, success, and engagement, internally and externally.

Notes

1. *Corporate Citizenship: Profiting from a Sustainable Business*, Economist Intelligence Unit (London: Economist, 2008), accessed March 27, 2016, http;// graphics.eiu.com/upload/Corporate_Citizens.pdf.
2. Howard Schultz with Joanne Gordon, *Onward: How Starbucks Fought for Its Life without Losing Its Soul* (New York: Rodale Press, 2011), 293.
3. As of May 1, 2016, Starbucks was in seventy countries.
4. Robert Richman, *The Culture Blueprint: A Guide to Building to High-Performance Workplace* (Culture Blueprint, 2014), 8.
5. Susan Waldman, "Small Business Advice: Brilliant Branding Lessons from Zappos," *Washington Post*, July 9, 2012, accessed March 27, 2016, https://www. washingtonpost.com/blogs/on-small-business/post/small-business-branding-lessons-from-zappos/2012/07/11/gJQAL2RPeW_blog.html.
6. Richman, *The Culture Blueprint*, 5.
7. Richman, *The Culture Blueprint*, 55.

CHAPTER 2

PROFESSIONALS FIND MEANING IN MENTORING

Forging Win–Win Relationships

My drive is the response from the kids. When you are the CEO of a company, the responses you receive can be artificial. There isn't real feedback. But kids are always real. When I am driving to school I think, "Why am I doing this? I am already so overcommitted." Yet, when I leave, I inevitably think, "Wow, that was really cool! Visiting this class was great!"

—Rick Toren, president of Atigeo, Inc.,
a medical software company

While chapter 1 focused on what motivates corporations to build mentoring programs, chapter 2 explores individuals and the meaning they find in building mentoring relationships. Whether you are a mid-level employee, an executive at the height of your career, an owner of your own company looking for deeper satisfaction, or you're a retiree seeking community involvement, you have a wealth of valuable experience to share.

Giving back is a journey of evaluating priorities, of deciding what you have to offer and how you want to spend your time and money. Of course, many organizations seek expertise, energy, and financial support.

In the 2014 *U.S. Trust Study of High Net Worth Philanthropy*, conducted by Bank of America, the findings show that donors who volunteered their time gave 73 percent more on average than those who did not volunteer.[1] The choice is about more than simply filling a calendar with commitments. The old saying "The more you give, the more you get" is abundantly true.

The goal is to find a cause that resonates with you and determine the role you want to play.

Over the course of our careers, we have each developed a unique and valuable set of skills, understandings, and experiences that have shaped who we are and our personal stories. When we share these stories, we sometimes don't know the ripple effect we set in motion. Our tales of obstacles overcome, resilience from loss, or strategy over fear can and do motivate others. That is why mentorship, as outlined in *Teach to Work* and other mentorship programs, can be the opportunity that allows you to find new meaning in giving and to hit your philanthropic stride. I have certainly found mine through mentoring in high schools. In this chapter, I will share my experience as well as that of others who have followed this same path.

Students tell us, repeatedly and in a variety of ways, that we are bringing something to them that they are not getting anywhere else. The mentor is an adult who is neither a teacher nor a parent but a respected professional who speaks from experience rather than theory, someone who does not stand in judgment and is not responsible for assigning grades or telling students what to do. Each of us is someone who says, "If I can, you can!" just by our presence.

Taking on a mentoring role as suggested in this book can help many of us feel connected, reenergized, and creative, as we give back what we know and share our whole selves. This is where our society needs to go if we are to help fill the skills gap in America.

Words, advice columns, and self-help books have far less impact on students than what they learn from another human being face to face. Learning means more when it comes from someone who has actually worked in the real world, survived, and succeeded. The combination of trained teachers, excellent curricula, and one-on-one time with a professional using this Project Based Mentoring model—works.

Marc Freedman is founder and CEO of Encore.org and cofounder of AARP Experience Corps, as well as author of four books. In *The Kindness of Strangers: Adult Mentors, Urban Youth, and the New Voluntarism*, Freedman calls for "a web of support for children and a portfolio of adults acting together, as partners, to help out with the complex process of developing young people,"[2] the tried and true formula where those with experience and well-honed life skills are connected to those in the early stages of seeking just those strengths. This person ignites a spark of recognition in a young person who dares to look at a successful adult and think, "This could be me."

Mentoring isn't so much about your job title or past positions, though these might turn out to be interesting and valuable. The most crucial characteristic looks like the most ordinary—it's simply you, or, more accurately, you and your willingness to show up. And by the way, it's you in your entirety—not just your record of success. It makes a difference that, alongside your achievements, you logged some failures; you were a student once, you didn't know what you were going to do, you struggled with math, lacked confidence, or maybe got into trouble from time to time.

Journey into the Classroom: My Story

My family formed a foundation in 1998. Life shifted for me from thinking solely about earning a living and supporting my own needs to thinking more broadly about society, and what we as a foundation could offer, where we could give, and the legacy we would leave. I took on this assignment with great seriousness and a sense of responsibility, after introspection and study. I was a new participant in a philanthropic foundation and I had a one-third vote on where and how to give. My involvements in philanthropy include being:

- Trustee of a family foundation
- A student of theological thought, focusing on the history of giving
- A board member for a multitude of nonprofits
- A participant at philanthropy seminars, including the Philanthropy Roundtable, Council on Foundations, Washington Regional Association of Grantmakers, Aspen Institute Forum on Philanthropy, Global

Philanthropy Forum, Small Family Philanthropy Association, and the Washington Area Women's Foundation

- Host of a two-year radio talk show called *For Love or Money,* which featured a one-month series on philanthropy
- A consultant to nonprofits on developing programs in active philanthropy
- Leader of a speaker series as a consultant for the Washington Regional Association of Grantmakers
- Creator of a Washington cohort for the philanthropy division of the Aspen Institute

Through all of these philanthropic pursuits, my personal experience of being a mentor for more than fifteen years with the Network for Teaching Entrepreneurship (NFTE) has meant the most. Why? First, mentoring allows me to give from my whole self. I not only support the organization financially, but I share my knowledge, creativity in business, and values with students. Second, through mentoring I can help realize the core of my belief system: that there is no higher form of giving than to help others open their minds to new interests, learn employable skills, and develop self-sufficiency. This deeply held sentiment stems from studying the twelfth century theologian, Maimonides, and his vision for a hierarchy of giving.[3]

Bringing Others In

As I mentioned in the introduction, my idea for this book was developed during my time as a board member for NFTE. Its nationwide program does a fabulous job of educating students about the core principles of business. Not only are kids taught to write and defend a fifteen- to twenty-page business plan (by a certified teacher within Title I schools), they are given seed capital so they can experience buying low and selling high. Indeed, many actually take a product or service to market and turn a profit. But the aspect of the program that captured my imagination was the extraordinary power of mentoring. I asked myself these questions:

- What value could businesspeople bring to the classroom?
- Wouldn't students be interested in learning from real people rather than from a textbook or theoretical model?
- Wouldn't teachers enjoy expanding the students' horizons—and their own—with real-world examples of struggle, survival, and success?
- Would it be possible to create a model that wouldn't interfere with the class curriculum or the teacher, and would also fit into the busy lives of professional people?
- How could we design a program with recurring visits that provided a meaningful connection for both mentor and mentee?

Personally, as a donor, I wanted to see and hear the actual teaching of the NFTE program I was underwriting—I desired a touch point with the organization beyond just funding it. I thought, wouldn't other donors have the same sentiment? So, it all started because I was a NFTE board volunteer with an expertise in marketing. I wanted to create something that would engage and sustain donor relationships and allow supporters to go beyond financial giving and share their knowledge as well.

As it happened, I wrote a proposal as a consultant, stepped off the board, and, with the blessing of the D.C. regional office of NFTE, began to develop a pilot mentoring program. That first year, 2001, I was a guinea pig, along with my co-mentor, Phil McNeill. Not only had I discovered a significant joy, but I realized we were onto something, organizationally. The concept for Adopt-a-Class was hatched and becoming operationalized. I became wholeheartedly convinced of the value of our idea after receiving students' year-end letters about the ways our presence had shifted their thinking or opened their eyes to new pathways (of course, we were adjunct to a teacher and an award-winning curriculum). But I realized this pilot was potentially a win–win–win–win, for students, teachers, the nonprofit, and mentors. At this point, I went to great lengths to recruit more mentors at the regional level and to expand the pilot to a national model.

During those first two years, I ran the program. Twenty-five professionals from different areas of business—including finance, real estate, technology, medical software, and investments—all funded a class, were trained, were introduced to teachers, signed an introductory memo of understanding, and committed to mentoring students for the full academic year. We made the schedule flexible enough that it could work based on the mentor's availability. The idea took off. A culture of volunteerism and mentorship expanded within the D.C. region, with first 30 percent and then 60 percent of the NFTE board members going into classrooms by 2007. By 2011 in Washington, D.C., there were more sponsors than classrooms we could place them in! Indeed, several publications covered the model, from the *New York Times* and the *Washington Post* to *Philanthropy* magazine. The "mentor culture" had also been received well nationally. By 2009, the strategic plan from NFTE headquarters ranked volunteerism as a clear priority, requiring some form of mentorship in every classroom in the United States. However, the unique Adopt-a-Class model, which included a financial contribution, recurring visits over a full academic year, and a Project Based Mentoring experience (a new term presented in this book), was successfully incorporated by eleven NFTE regional offices across the country (figures based on 2014 study).

As time progresses and new leadership takes hold, the original model has been improved; efficiencies have been implemented and regional adaptations made, but the overall concept remains for bringing corporate and business mentorship to students (see www.nfte.com).

In 2010, I was an honoree at NFTE D.C.'s annual gala because of my work with more than four hundred students over ten years. It was a pinnacle event in my life because ten of my mentees returned to Washington, D.C., from all parts of the country to be surprise guests at the gala. They were invited on stage for individual interviews and asked to share how "Ms. Patty" had touched their lives.

The keynote speaker at the gala that night was Chris Gardner, whose compelling life story about beating the odds was published as an autobiography, *The Pursuit of Happyness*, later followed by a film of the same name starring Will Smith. Gardner got up in front of one thousand people and said, "I had a whole speech planned, but I am sorry, I am going to rip it up. I want to talk to you, Ms. Patty."

Gardner said, "Let me tell you something, you are not only changing the lives of these kids, you are changing the lives of their kids. And, in my newest book I speak about *spiritual genetics*. It is something much deeper than bloodlines. These kids latch on to people they know they can trust, they can look up to, and that are giving them something they are not getting otherwise. Thank you, Ms. Patty."

This was a very public moment for a lot of years of very private work.

Touching Lives through Mentorship

Nothing equals the high of discovering that, through your actions, you have changed a life. The elation comes in all shapes and sizes: it can be through your regular interactions with the students, through reflections they share later in letters, or through relationships that develop over years. At times, I have found it hard to make it to class—it takes discipline to stop what you are doing, battle traffic, and drive the distance to school. You might arrive to find a class of kids who are tardy, challenging, unreceptive, and seemingly not taking in what you are saying.

Inevitably, however, *every* single time I leave the classroom I am on a high. Sometimes it is because of my deepening understanding of the simple but poignant questions students ask and sometimes it is because I've witnessed a lightbulb going off in their heads. Sometimes I am inspired by a new understanding; what I've learned about at-risk kids and how I'm less likely to think in stereotypes about low-income urban youth, as a result. My perceptions have grown more realistic, more nuanced.

The deepest part of the experience that keeps me coming back year after year is reflected in the letters I receive from the kids. Consider Kevin. To be honest, after visiting his class for three months, I had not even noticed Kevin. He stayed in the back of the classroom, seemingly camouflaged, deflecting any attention. It wasn't until the entrepreneurship teacher from Largo High School in Upper Marlboro, Maryland, paired us up for a one-on-one session that I met him, or even knew he was in the class.

We sat down at the scratched library table, far away from others who could overhear us. I introduced myself, as I often do with students at our first encounter, and explained that I was not there to tell him what to do. Quite the contrary, he was the businessman, and I was there to help him as a consultant. That meant that he would ultimately make the decisions, and he could take or leave my ideas as he saw fit. The idea was to give him complete authority but ample support. I explained that my job as a consultant was to brainstorm with him to figure out what would be best for his business.

After this introduction, Kevin handed me a completed business plan—and I was impressed. It was only January and he had already fleshed out many of the business details for his lawn-mowing business. I immediately praised him, saying, "Wow, Kevin, this is impressive. Most students aren't this far along with their plans, especially at this early juncture. What questions do you have? What are your obstacles?"

He could barely look me in the eye. His glance remained fixed on the scratches in the table. In a faint whisper he said, "Well, I just don't know how to get started. Besides, I have a job at McDonald's, and I don't know how to fit it all in."

I responded by validating his work dilemma. Not only was the lawn-mowing business not going to start for several months, but many entrepreneurs are conflicted by the comfort of a steady paycheck versus branching out on their own. I offered to help him weigh the pros and cons of each, and also to help outline a calendar for spring that might allow him to handle both responsibilities. Next I said, "Kevin, I can help you get started with your business, but first I have a few questions. Can you mow lawns? Do you have any track record? And do you notice a need in your neighborhood for your services?"

For the first time Kevin got excited, he actually looked me in the eye, and he said in an animated voice, "Yes, I'm really good at lawn mowing. I mow my parents' lawn every weekend, and it looks really nice. Beds are edged, the grass is even. And, I notice that many neighbors' lawns look terrible. I know I could improve their lawns' appearance."

"Okay, Kevin," I responded, "I want to role-play with you. I'm going to pretend to *be you* going door to door in your neighborhood." I took the NFTE textbook and pretended to knock on a neighbor's door, and Kevin pretended to be a homeowner. I said, "How do you do? My name is Kevin and I run Kevin's Lawn-Mowing Service. I am a student in Largo High School's entrepreneurship class. This is a copy of the Network for Teaching Entrepreneurship textbook and here is my business plan. I am experienced, as I have been mowing lawns right up the street here for two years now, and I would like to demonstrate the quality of my work for you today. Would that be okay? May I mow your lawn for $20? If you really like it, I would be interested in setting up a weekly contract. Would that be all right with you?"

I then asked Kevin, "Do you think you can knock on your neighbor's door and role-play this?" We switched seats, he knocked on my door, and we role-played again. He got it perfect.

We discussed the idea of a seasonal contract that customers could sign, which detailed weekly payments upon completion of work and established dates for recurring service. We wrote out a simple contract he could use.

The teacher told me Kevin came back into the class with a spring in his step and an actual smile. I returned to class in March, April, and May but only saw Kevin in the back once in all those visits. At year end, however, I received this letter, which almost blew me away:

Dear Miss Patty,

I really appreciate the time you spent with my class and helping us to make our business ideas and plans better. With all the great and new ideas you put into my head, I have already become a success in my neighborhood. I have eight regular customers already, and I have used the contracts you said I should. I am very proud of myself and have found that the advantage of gaining self-confidence is true when you own your own business.

You made us all laugh and you made us all think hard about what it takes to be a successful entrepreneur. I know I have what it takes . . . even though I did not compete in the business plan competition this year, next year I expect to enter and come out victorious winning the whole thing . . . Thank you for everything you have done to help me get started,

Kevin

Kevin quit his job at McDonald's. He was earning upwards of $200 a week and hired friends to help fulfill his contracts.

The amazing thing? Kevin and I had only one conversation. He had all this capacity within himself, but could just as easily have quit. Just a 'skosh' of 'how-to' was all he needed.

Some of the students I have mentored have later asked me to write a college recommendation, invest in their businesses, answer questions about life, or provide advice. You may meet students who have no real place to call home, who don't know or live with their parents, or who have parents who are heroin or cocaine addicts. The dynamic of the mentor–student relationship brings connection and value to these young people's lives.

In the following examples from NFTE's Adopt-a-Class program you will see how mentorship has deeply touched the lives of both mentors and students in ways that may make you wonder who is giving to whom, who is teaching and who is learning. What is certain is that both mentor and student grow, operate in a larger sphere of understanding, and prosper from this connection.

Linda Berdine: "One of the Most Fulfilling Experiences"

The high school students Linda Berdine mentors may not immediately relate to her success as an entrepreneur who has built three successful information technology companies (and sold two of them for substantial returns). They do, however, relate to her personal struggle: an only child who spent the first year of her life in a German orphanage, Berdine was raised by a U.S. military family of modest means. Her adoptive parents later made their living by running a small business, setting an example that instilled the early seeds of entrepreneurship within her.

"I always speak to the classes about my background, and I say, 'You are able to do this!' I did not come from parents who had wealth that could help me start my business; I did not come with a silver spoon. I know some of them have single parents that may not be as engaged as they would like. I want them to know that even if you have a rocky start you can be successful," Berdine said.

Berdine, who has been a mentor in entrepreneurship classes at T.C. Williams High School in Alexandria, Virginia, since 2011, decided to be a mentor at a time when she was evaluating what her next stage in life would be after great success in the IT field. She said she wanted to leave "some sort of legacy of knowledge for the next generation."

Berdine went on to say, "It became very clear to me that this was my time to give back. I had instilled in my company a feeling to give back to the community. So, now I asked myself individually, 'What do I want to do?' I wanted to help the students imagine beyond the bounds of what they knew. That is what happens to a lot of entrepreneurs, we imagine beyond the bounds of what we know."

In addition to helping students create business plans, Berdine loves teaching students practical things, like how the stock market works and how it impacts their lives. When Berdine shares her firsthand experience as an entrepreneur, students always want to know how she got started, what her first job was, and how she ultimately picked her career.

"They take you back to your beginnings," Berdine says. "I always pause and think, 'How can I turn this answer into a lesson?' I tell them my first job was picking strawberries in West Virginia, and that theirs might be cutting grass, but that could set the groundwork for them to become an entrepreneur."

Berdine also talks to the kids about failure. Pursuing success involves risks, and she tells them you can't win at everything in life: "This is a very valuable lesson, but that doesn't mean that you won't go on and be the most successful at what you do. You need to learn how to accept failure. If one of my clients cancelled a contract I can't just stop trying to build my company."

One student's experience that stands out is that of a young man named Dagim, who was a junior in high school when Berdine met him. He was initially a quiet student, but as the semester progressed he began to blossom. He came up with an innovative idea to develop an app that allows spectators to post comments in real time during high school sporting events—like a Facebook for high school sports.

Berdine helped Dagim draw up his business plan and calculate his return on investments, but in the meantime he was already pulling in peers, bringing in money by selling advertisements, and making high-level contacts who could help him find a way his app could be used in professional sports.

"I tell people it [mentoring] is probably one of the most fulfilling experiences I have going on in my life right now. It gives me hope when I work with these kids and I see their ability and creativity to start up initiatives; it is a marvelous thing," Berdine said.

Following is a letter Dagim wrote about Linda Berdine:

My mentor, Linda Berdine, helped me take my "first steps" in the business field. She taught me about the basic principles of business and the importance of networking. From the step-by-step help in the creation stages, through the entire process of building my business. Furthermore, her stories motivated me to join the entrepreneurial world as my own businessman.

(She) influenced me in both my business career, but also personal(ly) helping me reach my own potential.

Some things I took away from (her) specifically are the power of confidence and leadership in the business field. I learned that poise and conviction towards a business will lead to people's interest and investments. Additionally, my communication skills and confidence have greatly increased. I have the ability to present to large groups articulately and without fear. To conclude in gratitude, I want to thank my mentor for helping me set off my business career and dreams.

Phil McNeill: "We Made a Lot of Impact Right Away"

Phil McNeill is currently managing partner at the Maryland-based investment firm Farragut Capital Partners. He first joined NFTE's board of directors in 1999 when he was managing director of investments with Allied Capital, and he became more involved as a business plan judge over several years. After watching the kids in action at the competitions and seeing the organization from both an "organizational level and a kid level," McNeill knew things could be taken a step further.

"I remember going to one of the competitions and thinking, 'That was really good, but if they [the students] had talked to someone about their plans and understood the step-by-step process of starting a business, the business plans could be a lot better," McNeill said. Phil McNeill and I were on the board at the same time, and we were on the same page then, as we are now. So when I proposed starting the Adopt-a-Class program, I asked Phil if he would like to be my co-mentor. He said yes, and the rest is history. We are now in our fifteenth year of mentoring students together.

"It became clear there was a real need to go into the classrooms," McNeill said. "We made a lot of impact right away." Over the years, he has delighted in rediscovering time and again that "What you put in is a fraction of what you get out." McNeill's success as a mentor comes from his down-to-earth demeanor with the students and from approaching them as a peer and fellow entrepreneur.

"The fastest way to turn kids off is to tell them how great you are. We talk to them *as peers*. We have some experience and they have ideas, so we listen to what they have to say and trade off. We also talk to them about failures—good entrepreneurs fail at least three times. It is about perseverance, taking an idea as far as you can," he said.

McNeill enjoys dissecting the process of starting a business. "We help them take the initial steps, we help them break down the barriers, and we help them think through an action plan, step-by-step. We suggest before you have a restaurant, start a catering business. We love watching the lightbulb go off. We try to get them to go out and actually start a real business."

For McNeill, another draw to mentoring youth is passing on the entrepreneurial thinking and support he had growing up. He talks to the students about his path, coming from a small, rural town in Oklahoma. His dad died when he was just six years old and the family was "stuck." He feels fortunate that he attended a good high school, a good college, and then went on to earn an MBA from Harvard University.

"These kids have barriers all around them, economic, racial, educational, but we all want the same things. I let the kids know they have someone they can call or e-mail and see at the next class to talk about things they might not be able to talk about with someone at home," McNeill said.

McNeill was just that person for Clarence. A junior at Woodrow Wilson High School in Washington, D.C., Clarence started a simple business that turned into a huge success. He bought day-old doughnuts for twenty-five cents per doughnut each evening from a nearby grocery store bakery. He resold them on the school bus the next morning for $1 each. The kids would line up.

One day Clarence didn't show up and the kids were really upset. They had grown accustomed to sleeping a few minutes later and skipping breakfast because they knew they could buy a doughnut on the bus. Clarence discovered how much the kids depended on him and began to understand the concept of supply and demand. It was a breakthrough moment. Clarence understood his value, as customers were willing to *pay* for convenience. He went on to win the regional competition that year with his simple theory and masterful execution.

"Clarence created his own demand, he was a bright kid, and I thought he had done a brilliant job on his business and I took an interest in him," McNeill said. He supported Clarence while he was applying to colleges, challenging him to apply to good schools and "differentiate" himself because of his business experience. He got accepted to Syracuse University on a full scholarship. There he thrived, becoming president of the student association and staying on to earn an MBA.

To McNeill, however, all the students have potential. "I think of all of them as my kids. We have our heart in the right place. We are not doing this so we can build our resume or to fulfill community hours. We get a lot out of it."

Clarence expressed his gratitude in a letter to Phil McNeill:

Dear Mr. McNeill,

As a result of your guidance and support I have learned a great deal. The biggest lesson in business was to educate your customers on how you can help them. As I continue my entrepreneurial pursuits in real estate development and management in D.C., I implement this philosophy, particularly in attracting new tenants and keeping the current tenants happy. Even as a teacher I use this philosophy to get buy-in from my students. It works!

I remember when you found out I was applying to Syracuse University. You were so pumped, as any worthy alumnus would be. Your continued encouragement through the application and decision process helped steer my life in the right direction. Indeed, whenever you came to Syracuse, you reached out to catch up over a meal. I'm so grateful for your consistent check-ins. It was reassuring to know I could always ask you for help and advice.

Thank you, Mr. McNeill, for all you've done and for your continued support.

Respectfully,
Clarence

John Lane: "I Never Could Have Dreamed of the Rewards"

John Lane, former president and current board member of Congressional Bank headquartered in Bethesda, Maryland, met Marcus when he was serving as a judge in a student business competition. Marcus and two other students started an aquarium installation and maintenance business called The Aquatic Kings. Lane was so taken with their business plan, he signed on to get an aquarium. That was only the beginning of a bond between the two.

Lane knows what it is to struggle financially, having grown up in a low-income household. He also knows that motivation is a crucial component of success. "I've learned it's important to be motivated by what you want and not by what you are afraid of," he said.

Lane has two daughters, so for him mentorship came naturally. "I never could have dreamed of the . . . rewards from being a mentor," he said.

The motivation and vision for possibilities that Lane provided to Marcus were what he needed to discover success. Marcus told Lane that because of their relationship he learned discipline, to finish what you start, and that making the right choice can be difficult. He also gained courage, because "sometimes it can be very difficult to be the only black person in a room."

Through the relationship, Marcus also learned to imagine the dimensions of new possibilities that could exist for him. After graduating from college, Marcus got a job as a teller at Congressional Bank and worked his way up to loan officer. He also realized his own dream to motivate other students, and is now a coach at Bowie State University in Bowie, Maryland.

"I could never accomplish anything better than seeing Marcus 'win.' My No. 1 legacy is that I helped to make Marcus's life better," Lane said. "But, I could only help Marcus because he accepted the gesture."

Rick Toren: "It Feeds Me to Watch Them Grow"

When medical software and equipment entrepreneur Rick Toren recalls his high school days, he remembers feeling like a "nobody." He was neither an A student nor part of the in crowd. Being a mentor allows him to do something he could not do as a student. It allows him to teach the kids how to differentiate themselves, not with a grade but by something they do.

Toren has distinguished himself as one of the inventors of the EpiPen, a device used to deliver epinephrine injections; as founder of CodeRyte, Inc., a medical software company that expedites transcripts from hospitals for insurance companies; and as current president of medical software company Atigeo, Inc., among other accomplishments.

Toren also has a contagious enthusiasm for business and an immense heart for the underdog, and is willing to carve out time to share his expertise. Despite all he has achieved, young people find him nonthreatening and humble.

Toren became hooked on mentoring after first coming as a guest to one of my classes, and has now been a mentor for ten years. His passion for teaching has led him to become an adjunct professor of business at Georgetown University McDonough School of Business.

"It is a wonderful investment of my time, and I am amazed at watching the change in the students. It feeds me to watch them grow," Toren said.

Letters he receives from the students in his classes say it all: "Thank you for helping me start my own business . . . " "Learning from you was the highlight of my week . . . " and "You taught me to speak in front of other people . . . "

Toren loves finding tactics to get the kids' attention and teaching them some of the life and business skills needed for success, such as looking people in the eye when talking to them, enunciating, being expressive, and using positive body language. Side by side with the classroom teacher, he helps explain to kids how to use a credit card, what assets and liabilities are, and how to create a balance sheet.

During Toren's second year at Suitland High School in Prince George's County, Maryland, he and Mena Lofland, an award-winning certified entrepreneurship teacher, motivated Andrea, his mentee. As with many of the students, Andrea had an inclination toward baking. Toren helped her define her market position, pushed her to be creative with her product and packaging, and encouraged her to sell, sell, sell. He instilled self-confidence in her and provided step-by-step guidance in developing presentation skills. Not only did Honeecakes Bakery win that year's business plan competition, Andrea was featured on the cover of *Philanthropy* magazine, cakes and all, as a flourishing high school student whose business was in the black.

Andrea wrote this letter to Rick Toren, to express her appreciation for his guidance:

Mr. Toren, you came into my life around September 2005 as the adopter for my NFTE Entrepreneurship class. I, a young, talkative junior, had no idea what I was getting into taking this course, but I remember your bubbly spirit and willingness to stay late and help students with our business plans. For a 15–16 year old to use terminology such as "return on investment" or "economics of a unit," appeared as a foreign language, however, Mr. Toren, you broke things down in a way we all could understand. Your relationship with my business, Honeecakes Bakery, is special not only for the assistance in creating and presenting a 28-page business plan, but you were also my very first customer with a purchase of a sweet potato pie. (Yes, I remember!!!) What makes you special is that your mentoring did not cease once I graduated from the NFTE program. We'd e-mail not only about the bakery, but about grades in school, or finding my first job, or just how I am . . . If I called you tomorrow you'd answer "Honeecakes, how's business?" It's a beautiful thing knowing that I can confide in my NFTE mentor to seek advice on running and maintaining my business. I am so thankful for the role you, Mr. Toren, have played in my professional life. You've gone above and beyond as far as what a mentor should be and I will be forever grateful for the role you have played in the success of Honeecakes Bakery!

Andrea

John Hasenberg: "I Was Always Rooting for Him"

John Hasenberg, a senior vice president at Merrill Lynch, accompanied me on a visit to Woodrow Wilson High School in Washington, D.C., his alma mater and mine, and discovered that mentoring in a local public school "ignited a flame" in him, creating a perfect opportunity to give back.

The kids took to Hasenberg, who had graduated fifteen years earlier, and who had a knack for connecting with them on topics such as pop culture, music, and the city's mayor, as well as business and world events. He stressed to them the importance of knowing what is going on around you.

"It is a rare opportunity to have the possibility of really changing someone's life, having a positive impact," said Hasenberg, who helped one of the students, Andre, get a summer internship at A.G. Edwards, Inc., the company he was working for at the time. Andre "blew them all away" with his energy and hard work. He did everything with precision and began to shadow Hasenberg at board of trade events.

Although Andre was only an average student, he had high ambitions and developed a strong work ethic from working with Hasenberg. After graduation, Andre was admitted to Morehouse College in Atlanta. Because of his mother's low credit rating, however, he did not qualify for a student loan. Hasenberg and his wife stepped up to cosign the loan, which Andre paid back in full.

"I was always rooting for and believing in him," said Hasenberg, who now regards Andre as one his most valued friends. For Andre, Hasenberg was the father he didn't have, an adult he could count on and go to for advice.

Andre has gone far since his days at Wilson. He attended summer school at the London School of Economics, became an analyst at UBS, a real estate analyst at The JBG Companies, and is now working for a private equity firm in New York City.

Ten years later, Hasenberg and Andre talk regularly and occasionally have lunch together. The tables were even turned when Andre wrote Hasenberg's recommendation for Leadership Greater Washington.

In a letter to John Hasenberg, Andre wrote:

John, over the past ten years you helped me get my first job, find a way to pay for college, and supported me when times were tough. To most people, this would be akin to a father–son relationship, or at least a relative. Yet, you were "only" a mentor.

Perhaps you didn't know that mentors don't usually fill the void of a father figure, answer the phone at all hours, or invite mentees to share what is going on in their lives. Maybe you didn't know you aren't required to say "yes" when I ask for a recommendation or a favor.

But it is imperative that you do know I am forever grateful. It's important for you to know that you've had an immeasurable impact on my life. And, I want you to know that when I think of you, it's not "only" as a mentor, but it's as a best friend, big brother, and godfather.

Thank you, John, for enriching my life.

Andre

Antwanye Ford: "If You Can't Visualize It, You Can't Do It"

Antwanye Ford, president and CEO of the IT firm Enlightened, Inc., and 2013 board chair of the Washington, D.C., Chamber of Commerce, met Chante at an NFTE business plan competition. He convinced the other judges that she deserved to come in first place for her business concept, Your Way Computers. He also knew he wanted to be her mentor.

Ford took Chante on as in intern in his thirty-person D.C. office, where she was a computer troubleshooter who immediately became well liked for her know-how and quick computer fixes. Ford had her write out a life plan—how much she hoped to learn and by when, how much debt she had, and whether she wanted a college degree, a family, and to travel.

"If you can't visualize it, you can't do it. You can't get on a bus and not know its destination," Ford said. "I have learned that sometimes I want more success for them (his mentees) than they want for themselves. They have to define their objectives and then I can help them achieve them."

After high school, Chante received a full scholarship to George Washington University. Ford helped keep her on track and focused on her studies.

Ford helped her launch her business by identifying government contracts, and he looks forward to partnering on future projects with her. "Along the way, these kids need affirmation, a pat on the back, and the knowledge that someone knows how hard they have tried. And, if you fail, you aren't doing it alone," Ford said.

Chante later expressed her appreciation to Antwanye Ford in this letter:

When I joined the Network for Teaching Entrepreneurship (NFTE) entrepreneurship class, I never imagined I would gain access to someone who would play such a major part in shaping where I am today.

Thank you for giving me a chance, for seeing potential in me and in my business. When we first met I was a high school student, just learning the ins and outs of being an entrepreneur and still trying to figure out what I wanted to do with the rest of my life. . . . The day we met at the business plan competition and you offered me an internship with your company changed my life. Antwanye, you played a major part in making my high school business, Your Way IT Solutions, a success to this day. You offered me a chance to prove myself in the real world, a chance to shadow you and be mentored by you.

By giving me a chance, you opened the door to opportunities for growth. All that you have done and continue to do means so much to me, I don't even know how to thank you adequately.

Chante

The writer Frederick Buechner describes a "calling" as "The place where your deep gladness and the world's deep hunger meet."[4] There's great wisdom in these words. To help us each tackle the "where to give" question, first we look inward to who we are, and where our "deep gladness" lies, then we ponder externally, at what is the world's "deep need" and how can we uniquely fill it.

Out of this reflection comes engagement—beginning to live out of your personal core values and find meaning by responding to a real-world need.

Recap

You have just read six stories that highlight a virtuous circle. By that I mean that the mentors you've been introduced to here have "paid it forward" by giving their knowledge, sharing of themselves, and doing so blindly. All they know is that they are giving their own life lessons and showing up. They can only hope that their gifts of knowledge and experience are received . . . but as you can see from their mentees' letters, they *have* made a huge impact.

In turn, many of the mentees, as we can see from their own words, are leading enriched, successful lives that they attribute in large part to having a caring, knowledgeable mentor at their back. Showing up is half the battle.

Notes

1. *The 2014 U.S. Trust Study of High Net Worth Philanthropy*, U.S. Trust Bank of America Corporation (2014), 5.
2. Marc Freedman, *The Kindness of Strangers: Adult Mentors, Urban Youth, and the New Voluntarism* (Cambridge, UK: Cambridge University Press, 1993), Introduction, xxvi.
3. Based on Maimonides, "Book of Seeds," Eight Degrees of Charity, 1178 AC; source: Jewishvirtuallibrary.org, "Eight Levels of Charitable Giving," accessed February 1, 2016, https://www.jewishvirtuallibrary.org/jsource/Judaism/Levels_of_Giving.html.
4. Frederick Buechner, *Wishful Thinking: A Seeker's ABC* (New York: HarperOne, 1993), 118–119.

CHAPTER 3

A STUDENT'S LIFELINE

Inspiring Students because You Did It and They Can Too

I know from my own education that if I hadn't encountered two or three individuals that spent extra time with me, I'm sure I would have been in jail.[1]

—Steve Jobs

Mentors hold a unique power to transform a student's life.

This has been my experience and my passion. I am witness to its impact firsthand with my own mentees for fifteen years. But in doing research I've learned that I am not alone—many others view mentoring relationships as central to education and human development. The more I learn, the more I wonder why it is not more universal as part of the American educational experience.

Experts are studying mentoring relationships around the world, and are coming to the same conclusion. Professor Urie Bronfenbrenner of Cornell University studied mentoring relationships in Japan and found that a one-to-one relationship between a pair of unrelated individuals, usually of different ages, can have a profound impact on an individual's development. He offered this definition: "A mentor is an older, more experienced person who seeks to further the development of character and competence in a younger person."[2]

In 1924, the French government created the Meilleurs Ouvriers de France, a coveted award that goes to 2 percent of a vast pool of applicants who enjoy exceptional skills in craftsmanship. The government program designates a select few as "métiers," or ambassadors of their special talent. Jean-Francois Girardin, vice president of the Société Nationale des Meilleurs Ouvriers, has said, "We must protect these métiers. If we lose all the brains in our country, we are lost."[3]

History provides important examples in every field of fruitful, even transformative, mentoring relationships: Socrates mentored Plato, Freud mentored Jung, Lorenzo de' Medici mentored Michelangelo, Haydn mentored Beethoven, Hammerstein mentored Sondheim, Miles Davis mentored John Coltrane, James Taylor mentored Carole King.

A 1927 study, *The Early Mental Traits of Three Hundred Geniuses,* found that mentors played a crucial role in the lives of one after another of the individuals considered geniuses in their field. More recently, in 1977, a review of Nobel laureates in the sciences found a similar pattern in *Scientific Elite: Nobel Laureates in the United States.*

In 1911, Frank Lloyd Wright created Taliesin, a school of architecture that had two campuses: summers in Wisconsin and winters in Arizona. (I never forgot touring this facility in the Sonoran Desert, not only because of its beauty, but also because of its unique educational footprint.) Students pursuing a Masters in Architecture had to attend year round for three years. Wright himself crafted the curriculum with the goal of creating the "architect of the future." Each student experienced a multifaceted learning environment with rigorous designs, critical thinking, and hands on projects. Students had to inhabit a shelter of their own making to experience their own design. All students were required to perform on stage and become adept at expressing themselves artfully. But, most importantly, Wright facilitated close relationships for every single student, not only with faculty and staff, but also with the adjacent architectural, engineering, and construction community near campus. Every young architect's studio experience incorporated a one-on-one mentor from the field.

Mentorship has become recognized in current-day philanthropic circles. I recently interviewed Rebecca Irvin, Rolex's head of philanthropy, and learned more about the Rolex Mentor and Protégé Arts Initiative.

Launched in 2002, and held biennially since then, the initiative revives the traditional method of passing on artistic knowledge over generations. The program pairs emerging artists from around the world with established masters in seven artistic disciplines—architecture, dance, film, literature, music, theatre, and visual arts—for a year of shared conversation and creative exchange. Each protégé, chosen by the mentor from a short list of rising talents, benefits from the senior artist's guidance for a minimum of thirty days over the mentoring year. A grant of 25,000 Swiss francs and a follow-up stipend of an additional 25,000 Swiss francs are given for a creative output by each protégé. "Over the years, the initiative has yielded some unexpected results," said Irvin. "Both young and master artist tell us that inspiration travels in both directions and that the relationship is mutually rewarding. We are also thrilled with the broad network of artists that comprise the Arts Initiative community worldwide." The list of mentor alumni have included such luminaries as Julie Taymor, David Hockney, William Kentridge, Robert Wilson, Philip Glass, and Alfonso Cuarón, to name a few.

Mentoring has infiltrated education as well. Most recently, in January 2016, Harvard University launched a training program for two dozen senior fellows from the School of Education. "The goal," said James E. Ryan, dean of Harvard's Graduate School of Education, is to improve the quality of classroom teachers in urban schools, create a model that can be copied elsewhere, and present teaching as a viable career."[4] The fellows will be placed in schools to teach part time, are responsible for two to three classes a day, and while working will have an on-site mentor as well as long-distance coaching sessions from Harvard faculty advisers. Katherine K. Merseth, who conceived of the program a decade ago and who is a senior lecturer at the education school, said, "You can talk all you want about teaching, when you *are* teaching is when the growth curve is the greatest."[5]

Meanwhile, in 2014 Gallup conducted various studies that looked at the links between education and long-term success in life and work. To give some context, Gallup has spent years defining a metric for the meaning of "well-being" in the United States and has extensively studied, measured, monitored, and improved on our understanding of this concept. The Gallup studies suggest there are five elements of well-being we all strive for:

1. **Purpose well-being**—liking what you do each day and being motivated to achieve your goals
2. **Social well-being**—having strong and supportive relationships and love in your life
3. **Financial well-being**—effectively managing your economic life to reduce stress and increase security
4. **Community well-being**—the sense of engagement you have with the areas where you live, liking where you live, and feeling safe and having pride in your community
5. **Physical well-being**—having good health and enough energy to get things done on a daily basis.[6]

Over the years, Gallup's studies have asked respondents to measure various questions about these categories on a gradual scale:

1. Thriving
2. Struggling
3. Suffering

In the United States, only 28 percent of the population responded that they were thriving in any of the five areas of well-being. That means 72 percent of Americans are either struggling or suffering.[7] Gallup and its partners designed additional studies designed to help organizations, communities, or educators to intervene and potentially solve the complex problems people were facing.

One of Gallup's studies researched education and its connection to work life preparation. It was the largest representative study of its kind in the United States and was conducted over the course of a year. Gallup interviewed one million citizens touched by education: samples of the general population, parents of fifth through twelfth graders, business leaders, teachers, superintendents, college presidents, principals, and thirty thousand college graduates.

During my conversations with Brandon Busteed, Gallup's executive director of education and workforce development and author of my book's foreword, he shared with me his rather remarkable outcomes. Gallup concluded that college graduates were twice as likely to be engaged with their work and thriving in their overall well-being if they (strongly) agreed to having any of six key experiences during college, which included the following:

- A professor who cared about the student as a person or a mentor who encouraged their goals and dreams
- An internship or job where the student applied what they were learning and a long-term project that took a semester or more to complete.[8]

Busteed emphasized the critical importance of both *what* students are doing and *how* they are experiencing it. These components in learning, Busteed said, "more than anything else produce engaged employees on a fulfilling career track." Yet only 22 percent of college grads surveyed said they had a mentor and only 29 percent had an internship where they applied what they were learning.

Busteed asserts, "*These elements of education are being achieved by too few. It should be a national imperative—owned by higher education institutions, students, parents, businesses, nonprofits, and government alike—to change this.*"

Mentoring Exposes Students to New Worlds

Mentors help pave the way for students' success but can also provide something deeper. Dr. Susan S. Harmeling, who holds a doctorate from the University of Virginia, undergraduate and graduate degrees from Harvard College and Harvard Business School, and is currently associate professor of business management at Howard University, has spent years studying and writing about the transformational power of entrepreneurship education. Her doctoral research has shown that students who are exposed to effective mentoring can be transported to what Harmeling calls "new worlds." The way Harmeling describes it, many students she encountered in her study of more than sixty inner-city NFTE students (from multiple states in the Northeast/mid-Atlantic corridor) are embedded in a particular, often disadvantaged, reality she calls "Place A," and although they may be exposed to "Place B" (a more desirable reality) on television or at the movies, in their minds getting to that place is unrealistic or unachievable for them. Those new realities are experienced only at arm's length and don't seem possible starting from where they are. When these students see Beyoncé, Mark Zuckerberg, Daymond John, or Barack Obama, they see mainly star power, not inspiration, because they cannot conceive of how they, or anyone else they know, could possibly reach such heights. Getting to where those famous figures are is simply the stuff of fantasy.

When those students are exposed to an adult mentor, however, one with a proven track record who is also accessible to them, a bridge suddenly appears between the two realities. The mentor may be a success but not necessarily a star. The mentor is human, not superhuman, as he or she shares a personal trajectory incorporating struggles, missteps, dead ends, and painful disappointments. Once the students hear a real person's life story, they can envision a new path for themselves. The story evokes the thought, "If he can do it, why can't I?"

Place B—where the successful adult resides—is now seen through a new lens. Harmeling says that it is through this process of "mentors actually being there and sharing, that students can be transported emotionally" and can begin seeing their own futures differently.

She first saw the benefits of such a program when working with students in an entrepreneurship education program in war-torn Croatia. There were few job prospects, and in that region young people lacked skills and often motivation. But their options broadened when they acquired some understanding of enterprise, and when they were exposed to mentors who ignited hopes that "maybe I can do that."

Harmeling notes, "Students who participate in project based, experiential learning with recurring mentorship begin to talk and act in new ways, and are able to envision worlds they have not imagined before. This is true even of students who come from a background filled with poverty, abuse, crime, and hopelessness."

Mentoring: Intangible Student Benefits

So far, we have shared historic and current research on the many benefits students derive from mentorship. After fifteen years and more than a thousand student letters, I can personally attest to the subjective, intangible gains that also prove beneficial. Following are a few excerpts taken from letters I received or from direct interviews with students. Note that the statements are verbatim, but the names have been changed.

Tiffany: "Whole Other View of the World"

Tiffany was a young lady who sat toward the back of the class at Largo High and mostly kept to herself. When we met, I could sense her skepticism and withdrawal. She worked with a group of gals on her jewelry business, and over time, the excitement of her project overtook her suspicions.

As complicated as the school year was, it was made much easier by you. With the help, knowledge, and down-to-earth friendship you provided, it affected me in a big way. Today there are rare occasions when you find people of such high standards as yours who are willing to visit, teach high school students, and enjoy it. Especially at a predominantly African American school where we are looked down upon with stereotypes and chosen to fail. What makes you different, is that you wanted and cared about us differing from our surroundings. With your encouragement I have walked away with the knowledge of running a business. Personally what I have learned thanks to you, I was completely unaware of in the beginning . . . Thanks to you I have found a whole other view of the world and the kindness of strangers.

James and Duane: "Leaves for Dinner"

After a rocky upbringing by a single mother in Anacostia in southeast Washington, D.C., and after several moves along the way, by their teen years brothers James and Duane were living in their aunt's one-room apartment with eleven other children, their mother, aunt, and uninvited mice. "Sometimes it felt like we were eating leaves for dinner, like all we had, basically, was a cabinet full of Oodles of Noodles," Duane remembers.

He and his brother James, however, enrolled in a NFTE class at Suitland High School and launched a T-shirt business with an emphasis on positive messages. They eventually contributed $16,000 from the sales of their shirts to help their mother buy a townhouse. And they earned scholarships to college.

Duane later wrote, "Before I won the business plan, before NFTE, I was skeptical in my attitude about business, I wasn't really valuing myself as much as I should. Once you believe something in your heart and you know you set out goals and you write things down, any idea and any vision, you could accomplish it . . . it's like power, *there's a great level of confidence just jump on you!*"

Gregory: "Slated to Be a C Student"

"Gregory is a C student. He's never going to be anything more," said Gregory's sixth-grade public school teacher to his mother, Sabrina. She reacted by scraping together funds to enroll Gregory in private school and getting him involved in several nonprofit programs, including A Better Chance and NFTE.

From the time he was eleven, Gregory had dreamed of becoming a disc jockey. He had a unique perspective on life, being both African American and Jewish. He saved all the money he earned from odd jobs and some he received for his Bar Mitzvah, a total of $3,000, and bought sound equipment, which he used to entertain his friends.

A few years later, a NFTE mentor told Gregory he could develop his hobby into a business: "You're a charismatic young guy. With a business card and a contract, you'd probably be able to DJ for some real parties."

"Just hearing, 'You can do it,' spurred me on," said Gregory. "That mentor was neither my mom nor my teacher, but a businessperson whose opinion mattered because he was objective and successful." Gregory earned more than $100,000 as a DJ in high school, dreadlocks and all. He grew comfortable with himself, his identity, and his success in spite of earlier doubts.

Ripple Effect

The students quoted in the preceding stories are just a few of many. Their expressions of gratitude are quite powerful, but nearly all the students have a similar response to an engaged adult who has achieved some success but who, like the students themselves, has experienced times of disappointment and frustration. A ripple effect is set in motion when students realize they share much more than they initially imagined with this creative and successful adult.

In making the journey from Place A to Place B, a student might rapidly jump from one identity to another, from being a wary, cynical, fearful student in the back of the classroom to a hopeful, engaged young person who feels proud of what she has accomplished and is confident of meeting the next challenge.

Recap

If experts, geniuses and Nobel Laureates benefit from mentors, if it is a model for learning that has stood the test of time, if it continues to be integral in

Masters and PhD programs, why isn't it more pervasive in the tracks of education where students need it most? How can we develop a robust corps of experienced ambassadors to pass on character and competence?

I am certain of this: students want to find ways to connect to a world that they suspect is quite different from either school or home. They need to feel connected to a world that looks complex and maybe incoherent. Instead of fear and rejection, boredom and memorization, a mentor's picture can offer an alternative pathway in a student's mind's eye, particularly for low income youth who need motivation, help discerning the next step, or insight into how to apply themselves with rigor.

I'm also certain of this: connecting with mentors can change a student's trajectory.

For that reason, I believe Teach to Work will transition the thinking and the methodologies of mentorship from being viewed as an act of charity toward being understood as an educational necessity—an act of true empowerment.

Having explored *why* we should mentor, we will move on in chapter 4 to look in depth at *how* to mentor.

Notes

1. Steve Jobs, "Excerpts from an Oral History Interview with Steve Jobs," NeXT Computer, 1995, accessed February 15, 2016, http://americanhistory.si.edu/comphist/sj1.html.
2. David DuBois and Michael Karcher, *Handbook of Youth Mentoring* (Washington, DC: SAGE Publications, 2013), 4.
3. Ann Mah, "Five Shops Where Artisanship Becomes Art," *New York Times*, October 12, 2012.
4. Lyndsey Layton, "To Build a Better Teacher, Harvard Launches Program Aimed at Quality," *New York Times*, November 27, 2015, accessed February 1, 2016, https://www.washingtonpost.com/local/education/to-build-a-better-teacher-harvard-launches-program-aimed-at-quality/2015/11/27/c445ef18–93b9–11e5-b5e4–279b4501e8a6_story.html.
5. Layton, "To Build a Better Teacher."

6. Tom Rath and Jim Harter, "The Five Essential Elements of Wellbeing," *Business Journal*, 2010, accessed February 1, 2016, http://www.gallup.com/businessjournal/126884/five-essential-elements-wellbeing.aspx.

7. *Great Jobs Great Lives: The 2014 Gallup-Purdue Index Report* (Washington, DC: Gallup, 2014), accessed February 1, 2016, https://www.luminafoundation.org/files/resources/galluppurdueindex-report-2014.pdf.

8. *Great Jobs Great Lives.*

PART TWO

How to Mentor

CHAPTER 4

PROJECT BASED MENTORING™

An Intergenerational Catalyst

I tell you one thing: if you learn it by yourself, if you have to get down and dig for it, it never leaves you. It stays there as long as you live because you had to dig it out of the mud.

—Aunt Addie Norton, *Singin', Praisin', Raisin',*
The Foxfire 45th Anniversary Book[1]

The mentoring relationship advocated in *Teach to Work* stems from work on a project. I believe a new learning dynamic evolves when a professional mentor teams with a student around a deep experiential (applied) learning experience. I call this: Project Based Mentoring.

Starting with chapter 4, we enter the "how" section of the book. Going forward, I will share a universal formula for designing a project, explore how to apply this formula to an array of student subjects and professional disciplines, and look at ways to implement the project. That said, it is up to you, the mentor, to take the elements provided here, use your own creativity, have fun—and apply this Project Based Mentoring framework either within your school setting or outside it.

The core idea is to unleash the vast resources and skills of America's professionals—incite a mentor revolution, if you will—to help prepare our next generation for the twenty-first-century economy. Essentially, we are teaching kids to work.

It is clear that, as a species, we are born to learn. We are lifelong learners. Follow a newborn through the acquisition of language, mobility, emotional intelligence, abstract understanding, critical thinking, and the mastery of needed life skills, and learning seems akin to breathing—we learn involuntarily as long as we go on living. But, unlike breathing, learning can nearly stop without causing an obvious emergency. We can find ourselves stalled, possibly because we each learn differently, we are bored, or maybe we find ourselves trapped. We are in a place where either we learn very little or we don't learn things we need to know that are relevant to us. Unfortunately, sometimes these places are schools.

This book is not an analysis of the problems in schools, nor does it propose a grand solution to the nation's educational shortcomings. But it does build on a well-founded understanding of how and why people learn. As the chapter's opening quote illuminates, a student's experience or integration with his subject is elemental to learning theory. We also come to understand that ideas need to be revisited or newly applied to today's challenges. Following are some of the many pieces of wisdom about learning that have emerged over the centuries:

- Teach a man to fish: the well-known Chinese proverb says if you give a man a fish you feed him for a day, but if you teach a man to fish you feed him for a lifetime. This proverb is about learning things that are central to living: survival.
- *Education for Judgment,* a classic by David A. Garvin and Ann Sweet, makes the point that two models of education have coexisted in an uneasy peace: teacher-centered versus active-learning approaches. The education reform movement's premise centers on the latter. As his book states, "Students must be invested in the learning process. They must care deeply about their education and the contributions they themselves make . . . too often class time seems . . . arbitrarily controlled and unresponsive to their desires."[2]
- In *The Fifth Discipline: The Art & Practice of the Learning Organization,* Peter M. Senge makes the point that, for most people, one of two beliefs

block their ability to create what they want: the first blocking belief involves being powerless, unable to bring about a desired vision, and the second is about being unworthy, not deserving what they desire.

- The famous story of "The Emperor's New Clothes," in which a child points out an evident truth, contrasted by adults who are obviously avoiding reality, suggests that young people are less likely to be constrained by societal influence and norms, and are more responsive to reality than adults.

- The Association of Experiential Education has a compilation of theoretical articles including Laura Joplin's "The Definition of Experiential Education," which begins, "Anytime a person learns, he must 'experience' the subject—significantly identify with, seriously interact with, form a personal relationship with, etc."[3] All learning first stems from the individual's relationship to the topic. Joplin goes on to explain that a generally accepted truth must combine "action with reflection" to engender a complete learning experience.

What ancient and modern wisdom tells us is that learning needs to be connected to something that students understand to be important to their lives, something in which they are truly invested. The courage to pursue a vision, or even a modest-sized goal, is suffocated when people feel powerless (others are calling all the shots, so why bother?) or undeserving (what do I know?). Finally, anyone willing to learn directly from reality, rather than simply comply with a widely accepted narrative—as is the child in "The Emperor's New Clothes"—is in a position to make a difference.

Early in human history, learning was mostly connected to life and occurred in the most practical ways; one generation helped the next deal with the challenges of survival. Later, in more evolved societies, each generation helped the next begin to master the known mechanics of planting, harvesting, and building. Independent of any teaching theory, this approach was a mix of "Here's how" and "Now you try."

Education has evolved into a vast and complex sector operating at every stage of life, replete with specialties, student testing, fields of research, legal frameworks, credentials, unions, and overseers at every level of government. Amid the accumulating complexity, there have been persistent and diverse movements to strengthen the learning process by reintroducing elements that are experiential, life connected, and action driven. Under different banners, and with many important nuances and distinctions, these efforts have recognized that a depth of learning arises through *experience* that might well be more lasting and more widely adaptable than learning that comes solely from absorbing text.

The idea presented in *Teach to Work* builds on an established educational model known as project based learning (PBL). According to the *Cambridge Handbook of the Learning Sciences*, a respected definition of PBL involves these primary characteristics:

- **Students work to tackle realistic hypothetical problems as they would be solved in the real world.** For example, what happens to trash? Where does it go? Is it safe for our community and the environment?

- **Students have more control over their own learning than they would under traditional classroom models by actively formulating their own "authentic inquiries" in problem solving.** For instance, rather than reading about how garbage services have developed over the years, the student devises his own research model to uncover answers to a question in which he is interested.

- **Teachers foster collaborative efforts with community members to help students find solutions in their areas of inquiry.** For example, in traditional PBL the teacher makes the assignment and oversees all students. The teacher might suggest research or even set up a visit from a trash collection service, a county sludge official, or scientists in environmental testing who collect data about environmental damages.

- **Students begin to develop learning techniques and develop skills that otherwise might have been above their ability.** The environmental project potentially garnered so much interest from students that they might learn new skills, such as how to interview experts or officials, how to tabulate data, and how to communicate about the environment.

- **Students most often work solo or in pairs. For instance, a student takes ownership of her project and devises her own methodology, uncovering an unknown outcome.** In this example, a student might plan a field trip to Mount Trashmore Park in Virginia Beach, Virginia, to see how one community used its solid waste and clean soil to create two man-made mountains, two lakes, a skate park, and playgrounds.

Evaluation has shown that students who participated in PBL improved their problem-solving and collaboration skills, and that they had developed more constructive attitudes toward learning itself than they had previously held.

Teach to Work builds on the best principles of the PBL model with an emphasis on creating a product, a service, a study, or an event for which there could be real consumers, real outcomes, or real change. *Teach to Work* also draws from the considerable school experience of NFTE, which has reached more than six hundred thousand students nationally and more than two million students globally with a project based entrepreneurship education (2015 figures).

Project Based Mentoring

What *Teach to Work* adds to PBL and other well-tested learning models is an *outside professional mentor* to help guide a student through her project. The Project Based Mentoring framework incorporates a mentor who has a lifetime of experience and a commitment to share that experience with students through projects that will maximize their learning.

The inherent simplicity of the program is that it integrates multigenerational and culturally diverse people around something to "do." The mentor and the student together are thrown into a dynamic with a mutual goal, a timeline, and a framework. The mentor has vast experience in the project dimensions and content. The student is the idea generator, the responsible party, the driver of the activity and its execution.

PBL outcomes have been known to fall short when the skills needed to address the various challenges are too far above a student's abilities. A typical teacher–student ratio is usually one to twenty-five. We have learned that often the project discovery process requires greater input, guidance, and one-on-one time than a solo teacher can possibly provide. Additionally, students can experience myriad obstacles during the four to eight months of their projects' implementation. We have found that consistent input from a mentor is eminently beneficial for a project's successful completion and the student's ultimate learning experience.

If we return to the trash collection example, some students simply do not have the social skills required to reach out and interview a community member or businessperson. They might not be confident in their "science speak" and thus unable to clearly explain their findings. Or they may not have the resources to take a field trip. Whereas the task was exciting at its inception, the student lost momentum, managed time poorly, became disenchanted, or fell behind. Execution can be fraught with obstacles. Not all students know how to employ grit or resourcefulness to barrel through a project. What could have been a great learning experience can quickly dissolve into an embarrassing failure.

Imagine this kind of student having the benefit of a skilled mentor who works in the sciences. What if a coach helped the timid student role-play an interview? What if there was accountability for a student's progress, to help him adhere to a schedule? What if a knowledgeable source was available to answer questions privately for a student who might be too embarrassed to ask in front of others? Or what if there was simply an empathetic ear to listen when a student was scared, in over her head, or didn't know what to do next? These are the realities with which we are all too familiar. Having a seasoned professional offer guidance at these critical junctures can make a marked difference in a student's achievement, confidence, and motivation.

Integrating Project Based Mentoring

Teach to Work offers a framework for all spheres of learning—design, technology, social science, mathematics, journalism, and many other fields—and teachers and mentors in all these areas can use this educational mentoring concept to further students' real-life learning. Seasoned professionals from many fields could interact with students in high school, community college, and university classrooms, or could meet with students after school at mutually convenient times.

PBL requires students *to apply what they are learning to the real-life situations they encounter as their chosen projects unfold.* The student begins with an unscripted idea, then researches the viability of the basic concept, tests the market, and brings the idea to fruition, which demands the integration of different skills, many of which may be untested at the time the project is launched. For the student, it is a *process of discovery* during which she learns what outcomes arise from particular actions and inactions. Project Based Mentoring simply adds professional support to this experiential learning theory.

Choosing the Best Projects

At the outset, we would recommend that the teacher and the mentor together discuss an overview assignment for the whole class (see chapter 6, "Meet the Teacher"). As I've mentioned, the assignment needs to be broad enough that each student has latitude to apply creativity to her own project, based on her unique interests. For example, in the NFTE model the overarching assignment is that each student must create a business plan based on her own business idea that she wants to pursue, then she writes and defends her plan for that particular product or service.

Another example of an overarching, all-class assignment for social studies might be for each student to find a social issue in their own community. Students would determine how they could contribute through improving awareness or researching ways to effect change.

To maximize the experience, students, with their mentors' support, should invest time in choosing a project that will present real challenges but with which they are likely to succeed. The following criteria are helpful in making a good project choice:

- The project needs to be *central to the curriculum,* with the student learning the core concepts of the subject via a project. Example: The curriculum for social studies includes learning about an immigrant population, so a student project might consist of researching and writing a paper on Vietnamese business owners in a community. A mentor might be a journalist, attorney, or business owner.

- A good project should turn on one or more *driving questions* that push the student to encounter the central concepts and principles of a particular discipline. Continuing with our example: driving questions might examine the difficulty immigrants encounter when they try to adapt to American culture. This may entail researching different stories of how immigrants were challenged and what communities can do to be more welcoming and accepting of immigrants.

- The project must involve the *transformation and construction of knowledge*. Expanding on the example: a student may have never encountered an immigrant population before, and the project would require face-to-face interviews, site visits to business establishments, and a presentation of immigrant life stories to fellow classmates.

- Students should be prepared to *work on their own*, taking responsibility for completing tasks on schedule and seeking help when needed. In our example: a student might need to prepare a timeline for interviews and consider arranging transportation to various sites. He may encounter a language barrier or difficulty in setting up meetings, which might require a mentor's input on timeliness, help role-playing interviews, and advice on anticipating obstacles.

- Students should understand that projects aren't scripted in advance and they *don't have a predetermined outcome*. Example: potential outcomes from student interviews could create empathy for the plight of new neighbors, and could result in the student publishing a journalistic piece. Potentially the student's article could motivate a community to develop a welcoming agenda and to support newly arriving immigrants in their neighborhoods. All of this is unknown at the beginning of a project.

- Projects must be *realistic*, affect a real population, and incorporate real-life challenges with possible solutions. In our example, issues that students discover, like the loneliness of newly settled immigrants, could lead to a call for community action.

Such projects make learning relevant for students, perhaps stirring their interest in a new field or skill set. Successful projects lead to some new understanding of the world beyond school. Because projects integrate knowledge gained from the class assignment together with knowledge acquired through life experiences, students strengthen their capacities for absorbing new information and incorporating it with understandings they already possess.

Students must create a coherent oral and written presentation for their projects, building on their own understandings, experiences, and ideas. Because their presentations involve lessons they have learned in their projects, perceptions they have, or findings their research has unearthed, they often manage to present with far greater confidence than when they are engaged in what is essentially a recitation of material culled from published sources (simply reading and recitation).

Learning that occurs in the context of problem solving is particularly valuable. A student will retain a sense of the obstacle confronted, along with the process that led to the solution. The student will approach the next problem—whatever it is—with greater confidence.

What Is the Mentor's Role?

Mentoring a student through a project is a familiar dynamic for most professionals. In our professional lives, work assignments often revolve around project oversight, and those who are at more advanced stages of their careers are frequently called upon to guide their junior colleagues. Sometimes this concept is called skill-based mentorship—the context, the subject matter, and the processes all fall easily into the wheelhouse of the professional. One example of such skill-based mentoring would be an IT professional who is handily equipped to help a budding technology student develop and implement a new app. The mentor's professional experience, from product design and development to projecting budgets, timelines, and implementation, are all part and parcel of his technical knowledge.

Students are often initially excited about developing their own ideas, the advent of implementation, and the unknown outcome. But some students may have difficulty finding a meaningful quest and managing their time in a way that lets them complete the project. They often need logistical support and emotional encouragement to take their project to completion.

This is where the Project Based Mentoring approach comes in: it helps with these difficulties. The following are areas in which a skilled mentor can help steer a project to a successful outcome:

- **Choosing a meaningful project.** A mentor can be a sounding board for ideas, and can help a student discern whether a possible project is realistic, feasible, and likely to end in success. (See chapter 8 for in-depth, one-on-one coaching.)
- **Managing time.** A mentor can help students develop a realistic timeline and an outline of activities. The mentor provides "friendly accountability"—not as a boss or judge, but rather as an advisor.
- **Motivation and understanding.** A mentor can provide motivation when obstacles arise, helping the student make sense of them with practical suggestions and empathy.
- **Creating a logical argument.** A mentor is invaluable in helping students incorporate their findings into a train of logic that explains the project and why it should work. When students turn to building presentations about their projects, the mentor's knowledge helps to design a speaking template.

The Essential Elements of *Teach to Work*

Clearly, many organizations have their own mentoring models in place. *Teach to Work* can be a useful resource for learning, training, or expanding programmatically. Prospective mentors, new mentors, or ongoing mentors can pull from best practices, can relate to my fifteen years of mentoring experience, and from integrating a project into your mentoring dynamic. You will find many ideas can be hatched and new creative mentoring approaches discussed with *Teach to Work* as a catalyst for change.

Following are some additional programmatic elements I recommend if you are employing a framework from *Teach to Work*.

Financial Underwriting

Let's begin with the first unique component: *the mentor can pay to play!* This is optional programmatically but can be valuable for a variety of reasons.

From the Academic or Nonprofit point of view: it commits the donor–mentor more deeply. In a certain way, the businesspeople are more vested in the students and their project outcomes. They want to see 'their class' succeed. Schools and nonprofits like to know that mentoring can be a revenue source, particularly as administering mentorship can be management intensive at the start. Often schools want to incorporate experiential learning, but cannot afford the kinds of projects that allow students to research, go on field trips, or have dynamic year-end presentations. The academic or nonprofit institutional campaign would suggest to a donor–mentor that their contribution truly enhances a student's real life learning experience— it 'makes the book come to life'—and better prepares them for the 21st century job market.

From the Student point of view: it's been my experience that students who know that we have underwritten their class are more motivated to perform well. They have expressed a new feeling of being 'invested in' the process and wanting to do better as a result. This changes the student–mentor dynamic to a quasi-business relationship, where the student takes on a more serious responsibility for the task at hand.

From the Corporate or Business point of view: I have observed that when businesspeople consider investing time and money, they like clarity of purpose, a spelled-out time frame, and a defined role. I propose to you that Project Based Mentoring as outlined herein does exactly that. An exciting new dialogue can evolve between the academic and business sectors as a result—a new linkage that blends a financial component with a defined mentorship role.

A common question about funding is: how much is the contribution and what does it fund? The designated officer for your mentoring program develops the per class donation and determines how the funds are to be used. Of course, as I mentioned, the Adopt-a-Class model has changed since its inception, but when we first began marketing this model to active donors, one annual class contribution was between $10,000 and $15,000. How you work with those funds is up to your institution. Some ideas include covering programmatic expenses for:

- Project materials (determine an allowance per student)
- Project research
- Field trips (transportation, meals, and so forth)
- Presentation preparation: copies, materials, posters
- Awards for the competition
- Year-end celebration lunch
- Stipend for teacher (if allowed)
- Resources and administration, such as for training and monitoring mentors

Project Design

The materials related to designing a project need to be distributed to the students at the beginning of the semester, but how does a student select a project? Working collaboratively, the mentor and teacher brainstorm ideas and then outline the terms of the class assignment, incorporating these elements (see also chapter 6).

- What is the mentor's particular expertise?
- What is the teacher's priority for the class?
- Does the assignment have alignment with the class curriculum?
- How would the project fulfill a real need?
- Will the project incorporate a field trip, guest speakers, and a fair competition?
- Is there room for the student's individuality to emerge?
- How will a student's project affect her overall class grade?
- What skills will the project help foster in the student?

While the professional has a good understanding of the field and best practices, the teacher understands the school culture, how students learn best, and what fits the curriculum.

All projects should include:

- A goal that is broad enough in scope to allow students to be creative
- A learning objective and tasks aligned with the objective
- A defined timeline and due date (three months, six months, or up to a full school year)
- Criteria for judging the project that are clear to the mentor and students
- A handout for students that defines the assignment and competition requirements
- Specifics for delivery of student presentations (for example, orally with a PowerPoint presentation, visually with a sample template or diagram, written in essay form, or through role-playing or reading)

Assignment/Presentation

The elements listed below can be used to focus the assignment, and also as part of the student's project presentation or paper. These can easily be adapted into a PowerPoint presentation with seven standard slides and at least five creative slides (optional). A written essay might also accompany the project.

- *Problem:* The student states the problem or need the project is addressing.
- *Objective:* The student explains the purpose of the project and how it will address the stated problem.
- *Audience:* The student identifies the primary and secondary audience the student is reaching, using demographic research. The student should be able to describe the project's anticipated impact on people or communities.
- *Implementation:* The student presents a timeline of activities, research, interactions, interviews, and/or experiments that are necessary for launching the project.
- *Obstacles/objections/competition:* The student describes problems that occurred in the course of the project's implementation.
- *Result/impact:* The student states a conclusion, explaining what the project has proven, how it has or hasn't fulfilled the stated objective, and how it has impacted the designated audience. There should be tangible proof of results, if possible.
- *Lessons learned/takeaways*: The student states what she learned through-out the project, noting what she could have done differently and how she might apply any new skills in the future.

Recap

Teach to Work is about preparing students for the workforce. This chapter suggests that an intergenerational, intercultural mentoring relationship can be enhanced by introducing a project as the didactic catalyst. Most impor-tantly, it focuses on students cultivating a real-world experience with guid-ance from you as the mentor.

Following is a list of potential work skills students can gain from this project based experience:

Student Assignment	Skills Gained
Project identification	Critical thinking, filling a need
Project master plan	Timeline organization, forecasting
Research/design	Adaptability, assessing market-driven change
Logistics/implementation	Strategy, integration
Periodic check-in	Accountability, follow-up
Problem solving/obstacles	Resourcefulness, collaboration, mentoring
Oral defense	Logic, public communication
Impact	Real-world measurement

Having a project for a mentee and mentor to focus on can create long-term benefits for both. Working toward a strategic project goal can be fulfilling for the mentee as he continues to progress, build confidence, and learn applicable work skills for his future. For the mentor, she enjoys seeing her guidance be put to good use, see the next generation learn from her experience, and potentially build a pipeline of skilled future employees.

Notes

1. Aunt Addie Norton, *Singin', Praisin, Raisin': The Foxfire 45th Anniversary Book*, edited by Joyce Green, Casi Best, Foxfire Students (New York: Anchor Books, 2011), 489.
2. Roland C. Christensen, David A. Garvin, and Ann Sweet, *Education for Judgment the Artistry of Discussion Leadership* (Boston: Harvard Business School Press, 1991).
3. Laura Joplin, "On Defining Experiential Education," *Journal of Experiential Education*, 4, no. 1 (1981): 17.

CHAPTER 5

RULES OF ENGAGEMENT

Establishing Expectations and Parameters

Never doubt that a small group of thoughtful, committed citizens can change the world: indeed it's the only thing that ever has.[1]

—Margaret Mead

I've written this chapter for you, the *new* mentor. First, because I've been in your shoes—and second, because I've introduced countless new mentors to their very first school experience. I know that you need to be prepared for this cultural journey in order to be effective. Nonprofits like NFTE and others or the schools who you might work with, will have their own "rules of engagement," but I wanted to take license and share my broad brush overview, my personal recommendations and highlights drawn from a variety of mentoring websites and manuals.

When I first visited my alma mater to begin research on the NFTE model twenty-five years after I had graduated, to be honest, I experienced culture shock. I knew immediately that the high school experience had changed radically since I had attended Woodrow Wilson High in the 1970s. A few of the changes I noticed follow:

- Security guards were stationed at the school's entrances and exits.
- Students were predominantly from minority and ethnic populations.
- Headsets, portable CD players, and cell phones were omnipresent.

- Super-baggy jeans or supertight jeans, depending on the sex, were the dress of choice.
- Police cruisers were present at the back of the building.
- Loudspeaker announcements frequently interrupted the classes in session.
- Students sauntered into their classrooms ten or fifteen minutes after the actual teaching began.

After seeing all of this, I quickly realized how much working in the business world had influenced my behavior and that of the people around me. When I attended a corporate meeting, people arrived promptly and paid attention. A stated purpose for the meeting was evident, leadership was clearly demonstrated, and action items with timelines were defined.

None of this seemed to be happening at Woodrow Wilson High. I immediately knew that, to succeed, each culture—school and corporate—needed to prepare for the other. To accomplish this, we had to define the business mentor's role in relation to the teacher's role and the classroom. We would start by setting clear guidelines; creative adjustments would come later. These parameters are also critical for a successful mentor experience. Following is a broad overview for how a mentor might interact with a classroom teacher, mentee, and nonprofit curriculum provider.

Setting the Rules of Engagement

For mentoring to work within an education environment, I believe several key members of the school and nonprofit teams should participate. These include:

- Mentor
- Classroom teacher
- Students
- Nonprofit/curriculum provider

Exactly what are the rules of engagement for a mentor entering a high school, community college, or university classroom?

Mentor qualifications might include:

- Excellent communication skills
- A successful track record in the business or corporate world and enjoyment in that role
- An understanding of the value of mentoring
- Deep concern about education and gratitude for being in a position to help
- A pioneering, hardworking spirit and a penchant for action
- The temperament to work with students and enjoy the experience
- Willingness to commit to a minimum number of visits each semester or school year

The mentor's responsibilities should be outlined and might include:

- Acting as an adjunct partner with the teacher
- Speaking in class on his or her area of expertise and inviting occasional guest speakers
- Mentoring individual students on their projects
- Helping prepare students for oral presentations
- Hosting a field trip, if possible
- Judging a project competition among the students

The mentor's expected classroom conduct should be spelled out and would include:

- Being respectful of the teacher and his class
- Being reliable in keeping appointments
- Understanding the need to set boundaries in relationships
- Listening and adding experiential knowledge to students and as a peer to the teacher

- Exhibiting perseverance and patience in the classroom
- Acting as a positive role model in dress and decorum

The mentor's ethical duty should include:

- Refraining from lending money to students
- Avoiding contacting students in person outside of school settings
- Copying the teacher and/or nonprofit agency in all e-mail communication
- Discouraging romantic gestures
- Maintaining a business-friendly tone
- Never permitting alcohol or illegal drug use among the students

Mentors should expect that the nonprofits, schools, or state agencies that bring any adults into school settings are required to conduct *criminal background checks* on those individuals. This is particularly important for visitors who are given recurring visitor status.

Expected—Policies and Practices of the Program

Mentors should keep in mind the following parameters, which I have learned over the years I have volunteered in high schools:

What is the timetable for your tenure as a mentor?

- An agreed-upon number of visits should be established at the outset of the school year or semester. This is based on the volunteer's schedule and availability. My experience (this is not NFTE's standard operating procedure, but based on my own fifteen years in the classroom) suggests that it is important to communicate a schedule and have it signed off on by the teacher and the mentor. This way they both know when the visits will be occurring and are committed. (I

typically visit about eight to ten times in a semester, to give you a
benchmark.)

- The teacher and mentor share contact information and logistics.
- The teacher and mentor also discuss school closings, snow dates,
  emergencies, and other possible contingencies that affect the planned
  timetable, as well as a communication plan.

An alternative plan would go into effect if the mentor is unhappy with
the school experience, the participating teacher gets terminated, or unfore-
seen emergencies arise. It is up to the associated nonprofit or state agency to
spell out eventualities through statements such as these:

- If the mentor has to drop out, a surrogate could be appointed.
- If the teacher has to leave, the mentor could be moved to a different
  school.

The Mentor's Relationship to the Teacher

If you are a mentor entering any school environment, it is important for you
to establish a rapport with and respect toward your teacher. The classroom
is her domain, and the mentor is a scheduled visitor who brings real-life
experience to the fore and works primarily with students on a one-on-one
basis (more on that in chapter 6). It is important for the mentor to honor
the teacher's knowledge and authority, both privately and publicly. As a
mentor, you might:

- Offer praise for the way the teacher manages her class
- Become acquainted with the teacher, inquiring how to best complement her work and letting her know what experience you bring to the
  table
- Periodically review your observations about your mentees with the
  teacher, to keep her in the loop

- Ask the teacher how you are doing in your role and how you might improve
- Be cognizant of the teacher's workload and curriculum timetable
- Ask for the teacher's curriculum and schedule of topics so you can align your contribution with them

Who pairs the mentor and the teacher? The nonprofit, corporation, or the school's development team does this. Meanwhile, you can better understand the selection process by asking questions such as:

- How does a teacher become eligible to host a mentor?
- How is it determined which mentor is right for which teacher?
- How much experience has the teacher had teaching in this subject area?
- How many students are typically enrolled in this class?
- Are the students required to be in the class or is it an elective?
- How will the school administration or nonprofit support the mentorship experience?
- Who is my point of contact, in case I have a problem?

Being a Mentor—Three Options

How well do you know yourself? As a mentor, how would you work best in a classroom? From our experience, mentors can choose among three options. Consider the one that suits you best: going solo, co-mentoring, or working with a corporate team mentorship group.

Option 1: Going Solo

Those who choose the solo mentor option tend to be extremely entrepreneurial in their outlook. Pioneers by nature, they're natural-born teachers. For example, Verne Harnish was one of the first mentors in the program. Not only was he a former national board member of NFTE and chairman of Gazelles, Inc., a global executive education and coaching company, he's the founder of the Entrepreneurs' Organization (EO) and a regular columnist for *Fortune* magazine. His syndicated column, "Growth Guy," targets venture capitalists. When it comes to public speaking, coaching one on one, and sharing business stories and best practices, Harnish excels.

I know, however, of one time he got rattled. On his first visit to an urban high school in Anacostia, a neighborhood in southeast Washington, D.C., Harnish was shocked to learn the school had *no* walls. Yes, a classroom without walls! Harnish was so disheartened by the environment, the amount of disruption he saw among students, and the lack of focus that he called NFTE's founder and ranted for forty-five minutes. Within a week, he'd contacted a furniture manufacturer that provided portable wall systems. Using investments and arm-twisted contributions, he hired the manufacturer to install wall systems for this entrepreneurship class. Harnish stayed on as a solo mentor for the full year, and the students reaped the benefits.

As a potential mentor, consider your own comfort with entering new environments and embarking on new educational relationships. Discuss your feelings at length with others and, after you visit the school, get a sense of whether mentoring solo will be a good fit for you.

Option 2: Co-Mentoring

Sharing the mentoring experience has been my favorite route. I've enjoyed having a collaborator, particularly one such as Phil McNeill, whose skills complement mine. McNeill and I have been co-mentors through NFTE since 2001. McNeill's Harvard MBA has given him an appreciation for the case study method of learning. Because he is originally from Oklahoma, he exudes that refreshing yet humble Midwestern charm and, as a dedicated entrepreneur, McNeill understands business plans to the nth degree. Today, his expertise in finance and strategy is constantly put to the test as a venture capitalist.

McNeill's talents complement my marketing, sales, and presentation skills. It is easy for me to create games and get students excited as they play with the concepts of market strategy and packaging. McNeill and I comfortably share the floor when we offer seminars. Plus, when either of us has a schedule conflict, we can turn to our co-mentor as backup.

If you are an independent entrepreneur, are a retired executive, or are near the end of your career and want to give back, this collaborative mentoring experience could be highly rewarding for you.

Option 3: Corporate Mentoring

Corporate mentoring requires a single point person. If you can garner company-wide interest, you may wish to enlist other recurring participants to join you and come to class, particularly when you set a mutually agreed schedule at the start of the class. An alternative is for the key person to be the one consistent visitor to the class, and assume the role of logistics coordinator for periodic visits from colleagues. (I weigh in on the side of recurring visits and in-depth relationships with students, but this is not always possible. All efforts are valued and beneficial.) For example, one venture capital firm had been a big corporate mentor for many years in the NFTE program. Its main representative came to the class repeatedly and included other company representatives in a variety of ways. Here are a few examples:

- **Classroom coaching.** Representatives worked one on one with students to help them create business plans. The professionals also helped with computer research and examined students' financials.
- **Classroom speaking.** When the teacher needed real-life examples, representatives of the company came in and shared their stories, problems, struggles, and victories in the areas of sales, manufacturing/distribution chains, finance, legal, and so forth.
- **Consulting on business etiquette.** On occasion, representatives from the human resources department visited to discuss job interviews, dress code, and appropriate professional behavior while describing what they look for when hiring new employees.
- **Hosting at headquarters.** The venture capital firm frequently hosted the regional business plan competitions, and students were invited to

its downtown Washington, D.C., office building. Employees saw the students visiting; some even sat in on the students' presentations and award ceremonies. This experience gave the employees a sense that their company was supporting its community.

- **Judging the competition.** Investment representatives from the host company were invited to judge the students' business plan competitions as well as to interact with them and ask questions about the companies they wanted to create.

Time Allocation

As you will read later in the book, your one-on-one time with students is the most valuable time you will spend. We recommend that these meetings be held outside the classroom, either in the school library or in a nearby office, which allows the teacher or professor to carry on with his course. The teacher designates which students will meet with the mentor at each visit and creates a student sign-up sheet.

The question remains, how much time do you spend with students one on one? This depends completely on the circumstance and the contributing factors. It is up to you and the teacher to determine how you can most effectively and efficiently spend your valuable time. Your plan should work for you and be flexible enough that it can accommodate your schedule. You are contributing your time, after all! Determining factors include:

- Number of students in the class
- Time allotted for each class
- Mentors' schedule and number of visits per month
- Number of mentors available

We have tried several different scenarios. The one constant I can guarantee is that no time ever feels like enough. As I mentioned earlier, my schedule typically calls for about eight to ten visits a semester (sixteen to twenty a year), so I have adequate touch points with each student on a recurring basis. It is my belief that this is where the rubber meets the road and where you can really help students achieve, if you only have the time. (That said, I do not want to represent NFTE inaccurately; as they scale in 2016, mentoring for this quantity of time is not standard practice any longer in the new Adopt a Class model.)

Of course, the precise allocation of time is a mentor's prerogative. Every person's time and availability are different. Discuss your scheduling needs with the teacher or nonprofit and decide what is feasible.

Teacher–Mentor Understanding

After you read about mentorship, you will want to draw up a memo of understanding between you and the nonprofit or academic institution based on your mentor commitment. You can review chapter 5 on the "Rules of Engagement" to help create this memo of understanding. (Also refer to Mentor.org's Elements of Effective Practice for Mentoring.) It is also helpful to spell out an agreed-upon schedule between the mentor and the teacher (based on the classroom schedule) as well as a line of communication in the event of emergency. See the sample form below.

Mentor Contact and Schedule Form

School Name: _____

Semester Date/Year: _____

Class Subject: _____ Class Time Start: _____ Class Time Finish: _____

Class Building: _____ Class Room Number: _____

Mentor Name: _____

Phone Numbers: Business _____ Cell _____ Home _____

E-Mail Address: _____

(Note preferred method of contact for emergency or cancellation)

Teacher Name: _____

Phone Numbers: Business _____ Cell _____ Home _____

E-Mail Address: _____

(Note preferred method of contact for emergency or cancellation)

Semester Schedule of Visits:

Month: _____ Date _____ Date _____ Date _____ Date

Month: _____ Date _____ Date _____ Date _____ Date

Month: _____ Date _____ Date _____ Date _____ Date

Month: _____ Date _____ Date _____ Date _____ Date

Included above is a tentative schedule of my visits to _____

_____ school.

_____

Mentor _____ Signature _____ Company _____ Date _____

Three copies distributed: mentor cc _____ teacher cc _____ third party _____

Your Role As a Mentor

It is up to you as a mentor to know what is expected of you in this role. Once you have read this book and collected additional details about what is involved for the particular program you are considering, determine whether you would enjoy this role and could commit a semester or a whole school year to this program. Being respectful of the classroom teacher and her role is key to your success.

Part of preparing yourself to be a mentor is understanding how the school's culture is different from the culture you probably experienced in your school days. It is important to complete your program's training program so you fully understand your role. Be prepared to sign a memo of understanding between you and the entity that brought you together, and develop a communication plan and schedule of visits with your assigned teacher. Consider your options. Based on your available time and your preferences, you can go solo, be a co-mentor, or take on the role of a corporate team leader/coordinator who recruits others in the corporation to participate as mentors.

Recap

I will leave you with this letter that I received from a teacher after I took her class on a field trip to New York City:

Dear Ms. Alper,

Thank you so much for the opportunity to take our students to New York to see the Stock Exchange in action and to buy products from the Wholesale District. That one experience has taken the class to another level of understanding business concepts. Nothing else could have done that. They understand "buy low and sell high" and profit and loss. They know now that everything that sounds good on paper is not always something [that] sells. For students who thought the selling experience would be easy, they found it harder than expected; for those who thought it would be difficult, they found it easier than expected. As a result, they came away with a greater respect for business people.

Many people have ideas about how to teach students, but you truly put "your money where your mouth is." Because you did, you have made a difference in the lives of young people. You have touched the future in a positive way.

I thank you for allowing me to be a part of this life-changing experience and for giving our students a chance to dream "outside of the box."

Sincerely,
Entrepreneurship Instructor
Kensington, Maryland

Note

1. Margaret Mead and Robert B. Textor, *The World Ahead* (New York: Bergahn Books, 2005), 12.

CHAPTER 6

MEET THE TEACHER

Setting the Course

Our partnership means so much to me and has made me a better teacher. The time you give to us is so appreciated; you have no idea the impact you have not only on me, but also our students. Your constant support in helping me to expand the program at Wakefield High and your participation in recruiting administration to get on board has been fantastic. The success of this class is most certainly due to you and your dedication to us.
—Maureen Naughton, NFTE teacher,
Wakefield High School, 2014

Between 2001 and 2016, I have had the great pleasure of working in NFTE classrooms not only in Broward County, Florida, but also in seven schools in the District of Columbia and surrounding areas, including: Woodrow Wilson, Laurel, Northwestern, Duke Ellington, Suitland, Wakefield, and Montgomery Blair. I have had to learn to work side by side with teachers and build a working relationship that is adjunct and that does not interrupt their classroom domain. That said, the NFTE teachers are quite different than teachers I am describing in this chapter, because they have already been fully trained and certified and the classroom assignments (writing and defending a business plan) are clearly spelled out within the NFTE curriculum. Therefore there is no need for conversations about content or student project assignments.

This chapter is taking elements of what I've learned from my own personal teacher-mentor dynamics, and adapting them for your use with other programs, other teachers, or other classrooms. How can you too, create a productive, working, adjunct relationship in these new environments that may not have a defined curriculum or project based student experience?

To start with, mentors are only occasional visitors, while teachers are on the front lines day in and day out. The teacher sets the framework for the students, establishes their expectations, and integrates mentors into the class workflow and curriculum. So let's "Meet the Teacher," as the chapter explains, and learn how to create this productive teacher–mentor relationship.

Bird's Eye View of a Teacher's Life

We begin by looking at a teacher's life, which is quite different from that of our associates in business. When you meet your teacher in August or September, at the start of the school year, for a get-acquainted session, you'll find it valuable to pull back the curtain and get a bird's-eye view of his life. You will understand why teachers deserve our utmost respect and appreciation. First, consider the numerous constituencies that our teachers serve. They continually juggle many balls while walking a tightrope.

- **Board of education**. Our teachers feel enormous pressure to deliver a test-ready class that meets rigorous statewide benchmarks in a finite time frame. These parameters are often shifting and in flux. Requirements trickle down into every classroom, and adherence and performance are scrutinized by boards of education and their constituencies.
- **Administrators, peer teachers, departments of learning.** Whether you are entering social studies, science, or English, rest assured there is a structure in place. School administrators manage hiring, facilities, funding, management, curriculum, and rules. Administrators are under a microscope from above by bureaucrats and politicians, from the margins by parents, from outside by patrols and security, and from inside by teachers.

  Then, of course, internal departmental structures review curriculum, teacher performance, and timelines. Our schools are community melting pots with big bureaucracies in place.

- **Teachers' constituencies.** Each teacher has to fit into this complex equation. Teachers report upward to the administration, meld laterally in departmental meetings, collaborate with peer teachers, and confer with vocal, often emotional parenting teams. The teacher is reporting student progress, behavior, performance, and social integration for each of his students (typically twenty-five or more) in each of his classes (usually four or five) multiple times a year.

    In addition to being educators, our teachers must combine masterful social work with the delicacy of public relations.

- **Students**. Finally, we have gotten to the main constituency our teachers serve: the students. The classroom is the special domain of teachers. They create the culture. They design the behavioral dynamic. They encourage civility and respect. They set the stage for learning. Though they are given parameters and curriculum to cover, it is Ms. Washington or Mr. Gutiérrez who will take our children to a place of curiosity and, hopefully, encourage an active growth mindset.

    As master schedulers, our teachers break down learning goals by quarter, by week, and by day. They spend the entire summer organizing a class's overarching path and then narrowing the focus to snappy ten-minute learning increments. Between literature, games, breakout sessions, and projects, they are artful managers who must convey masses of information and keep it interesting. When the school day is done, they are not finished; they must still review homework, plan the next day's agenda, or write tests.

- **Mentors**. As you can see, the teacher already has a full plate. At the outset, the idea of interlopers in her classroom could be threatening or disruptive. Some teachers are cautious about opening their private learning sanctuary to outsiders. Others have completely warmed to the idea and want more stimuli and support in content and experiential learning, and they welcome third parties with experience in fields other than education. If the mentor model incorporates a financial contribution, the teacher enjoys a budget that can be used to expand activities, purchase materials, and, potentially, as an additional stipend.

Either way, a mentor in the classroom may be new for the teacher, and represents yet another constituency to manage. This is important to understand when setting the groundwork for an introduction.

Where Does the Mentor Fit In?

Now that you have an understanding of a teacher's life and priorities, where do you, as a mentor, fit in? Your objective as a class mentor is to respect the teacher's domain and to collaborate with the teacher in an *adjunct role.* At the outset, your biggest priority is to get acquainted with the teacher, understand where she might need you, and follow her lead on where and when to participate.

Following is a list of ways I suggest mentors contribute:

- Offer input, based on your expertise, on the class assignment for student projects.
- Work with students one on one on their projects, during class hours but outside the classroom, in a library, nearby office, or cafeteria, or on an outdoor bench. After-school mentoring is also an option.
- Serve as a guest speaker and bring other guest speakers to the classroom.
- Lead one or more project-related class field trips.
- Coach students on the art of presenting.
- Judge the presentations in the final competition.

Meet the Teacher

Now the stage is set. You have a good idea of the teacher's priorities and the program. You understand your role as a mentor. It is time to introduce yourself. What happens at the first teacher–mentor meeting, step by step?

The goal at this meeting is to learn more about the teacher, and have him learn more about you as a person. When you get down to business, your goal is to leave with a clear schedule and contact information, and have begun a dialogue about the class assignment. Bring your calendar, your smartphone, and your ideas when you meet the teacher. (Going into this meeting, I like to know my travel schedule four months out—through the winter holidays, so I can book my visits for the full first semester at one sitting.)

Step One: Where and When to Meet?

The nonprofit coordinator or the development officer of the school will typically establish a time and place to meet:

- Find a time when the teacher is unencumbered and free to give her undivided attention. This may be in the early morning or during lunch hour, a planning period, or after school. A meeting could take one to two hours, considering the agenda below.
- Try to meet on the school premises, so you can become familiar with the surroundings, learn where to park, check in, go through security, and so forth.

Step Two: Who Attends?

The following are questions you might ask about procedures:

- Who determined this teacher was your match? Often, this relationship broker introduces you and the teacher by e-mail and sets up the date. This could be the nonprofit team member, or it could be a school representative.
- Depending if you are mentoring solo, as a team, or are the appointed representative for a corporation, determine which team members you would like present for this start-up meeting. Typically, it should include whomever will be present consistently and will be the ongoing point person for communications.

Step Three: Information Exchange

Establish a communication chain:

- The principal players, that is, the teacher and the mentor, need to share contact information, including: name, address, e-mail, classroom phone, home phone, and emergency phone. (See form in chapter 5, "Rules of Engagement.")
- In the event of school closings or the cancellation of meetings, what is the chain of communication? It is important to lay the groundwork for expediency, as this is often a point of difficulty.

Step Four: Outline of Conversation

The following is a suggested agenda of topics to cover with the teacher and diplomacy in embarking on this new, long-term working relationship. Set a relational framework of trust with open dialogue. Try to learn the following from the teacher you will be working with:

- His personal and professional background
- How long he has been teaching
- Whether teaching has been a long-term goal
- What brought him to the area and to this school
- Whether this subject has been an area of interest or specialty
- What makes this subject area challenging for students

Try to share the following about yourself, so the teacher can gain an appreciation for what you offer as a mentor and of how she might help in your interactions with students:

- Your involvement with the nonprofit and/or the path to your expertise
- Your school experience
- Why you want to mentor, your interests

- Any fear(s) you may have about mentoring
- Your strengths and areas of expertise
- Your weaknesses

To close the conversation and to be prepared for your mentoring experience, you might also:

- Ask if this is the teacher's first experience having a mentor work with her students
- Ask if she has any concerns
- If the teacher has a history of working with mentors in the classroom, ask about the pros and cons

You could say something like, "I'd like to learn how I can help you with your students. What are some of the ways you think I can best support you? I want you to know how much I appreciate this opportunity, and, you need to be completely honest with me about how I am doing. I don't want to overstep my bounds, and would like feedback, both positive and negative, from you."

You could also say, "As we get to know each other, you will find I have knowledge areas that are my strengths, such as [fill in the blank], and I am less knowledgeable in other areas, but I may be able to bring in other colleagues who have expertise. Would that appeal to you?"

Step Five: Schedule Your Visits

Confer and outline dates together, so that your calendars are set. Suggest that the teacher and you touch base prior to each visit. At that time, you can review the teacher's needs or the content to be covered.

Below is a suggested calendar overview to help guide your scheduling:

- August/September: Teacher meeting/introduction/project conversation
- September: Mentor meets students/leads class
- September/October: Mentor brings guest speakers and begins one-on-one sessions

- November–March: One-on-one mentoring with students, Teacher Sign Up Sheets: A teacher might offer a student sign up sheet to efficiently plot out the mentor's visit, or the teacher might simply assign which students will meet with mentors during given blocks of time. Occasionally mentors might bring in co-mentors, depending on number of students; mentor may be asked to teach a class
- April: Begin to hone student presentations
- May: Final competitive presentation/judging
- TBD: Field trip (during school year)

Step Six: Project Discussion

As outlined in chapter 4, the project scope is primarily up to the teacher to design, and potentially she will request collaboration with the mentor. The assignment should be achievable, be challenging, and teach skills that are relevant to the class subject. When discussing the project assignment, keep in mind the central components of project based learning, including that the project:

- Must be *central to the curriculum*
- Should push students to form an underlying *driving question* around a central concept or principle
- Should involve the *transformation* and construction *of knowledge*
- Should not have a predetermined outcome, but *incorporate an act of discovery* in the process
- Should *be realistic*, affect real populations, and include real-life challenges
- Should encourage students work *on their own*, taking responsibility for tasks and schedules as needed

Project Design Questions

The following section is laying out a framework for discussion about project design. As mentioned, this is primarily within the teacher's auspices, but it's good to understand the assignment goals and probe that they are met. Ask yourself these questions to discern whether the project meets the established criteria:

- Is it broad enough in scope to allow students to be creative?
- Do tasks align with the class assignment and teaching objectives?
- What is the prescribed time frame for completion?
- What are the criteria for judging the project?
- Have you prepared a student handout that defines the assignment and competition requirements?
- Does the project draw upon the mentor's expertise?
- How will the project incorporate a field trip and guest speaker?
- What are the parameters for the competition and how will student presentations will be delivered?
- How important is the project in the overall grade?

The project should encourage or require the student to:

- Engage in creative/critical thinking
- Develop a project for a specific audience and demographic
- Design a plan and a timeline
- Outline the steps of implementation, logistics, and budget
- Collaborate with a mentor
- Sharpen communication/presentation skills
- Present a case based on study and experience

Student Project Suggestions

The project assignment as posted to the student might follow this basic framework, which can also serve as the basis for the presentation:

1. **Problem:** The student should state the problem or need that the project addresses.
2. **Objective:** The student should outline the purpose of the project and how it will address or question the stated problem.

3. **Audience:** The student should identify the primary and secondary audiences she will be reaching, using demographic research. What is the anticipated impact or driving question posed to this audience?

4. **Implementation:** The student presents a timeline of activities, research, interactions, interviews, and experiments necessary to launch the project with a due date of three months, six months, or up to a full school year.

5. **Obstacles, objections, competition:** The student declares issues that arose during the research and discusses how these impacted their outcomes.

6. **Result/impact:** The student should make a conclusion, stating what the project has proven and how it has or has not fulfilled its objective. The student should also describe how the project has impacted the designated audience, providing tangible proof of results, if possible.

7. **Takeaway:** The student should be able to state what she learned throughout the project, noting what she could have done differently, and how she could apply any new skills gained in the future.

The student can be assigned to build a PowerPoint presentation and an oral defense of her case, project, or research with the above-listed seven standard slides, together with an additional five creative slides of her choosing. A written or pictorial essay could also be included with this oral presentation. Guidelines should be outlined by the teacher or project leader.

Project Grade

Finally, the project assignment should include the criteria on which the student will be evaluated during the competition phase by guest judges. Additionally, the assignment should make clear how important the project is relative to a student's overall class grade. The judging criteria are entirely up to the teacher, with input by the mentor. Consider the following suggestions:

- **Presentation.** Student presentations may be delivered orally with a PowerPoint presentation, visually with a sample template or diagram, in written essay format, or through role-playing or reading. Presentations will be judged according to how articulate a student is during his presentation, how strong the visuals are, and how clearly he explains the concepts.

- **Logic.** Hypothetical problem is based on a real-world issue, and the project design needs to make logical sense. Does the student demonstrate an understanding of the train of logic?
- **Audience/demographic.** A real audience was considered and potentially affected by the outcome of the project.
- **Research.** The student demonstrated rigorous research skills and offered proof of outcomes.
- **Implementation.** The presentation includes the methodology, timelines, and budgets associated with the project.

The formula outlined above can be adapted to many subjects, and is a format that is flexible enough to allow you to add your creativity. The table below offers a few ideas for projects.

Table 6.1 Potential Idea Match

Class	Art	English	Social Studies	Sciences	Math	Tech
Mentor Field	Advertising	Journalism	Law	Engineer	Accountant	IT
Project Idea	Retail Campaign	PR/Media Select Issue-LGBT	Community Project Social Justice	Environment Study, Water Cleanliness	Household Budget	Design App
Field Trip	Ad Agency	Newspaper Tour	Homeless Shelter/ Legal Aid	River/Field	Bank/ Finance Offices	IT Soft Ware/ Social Media Office

Ideas for Student Projects

When trying to help your student select a project, its valuable to see the end game first. Review the following examples, which are divided by class subject and professional sector:

> These project outlines are hypothetical for the purposes of the book, and each are written from the student perspective, representing their findings at the end of a project.

Example 1

Class: math, finance

Possible mentor professions: accountant, financial consultant, investment advisor, stockbroker, venture capitalist, businessperson, banker

Project options:

- Track a single product: reverse engineer to determine the cost of goods used in its creation. Do a spreadsheet taking the product through a life cycle that includes all costs associated with development, from manufacturer to wholesaler to retailer to consumer. Outline the financial trajectory through the process and track that product all the way through its cycle.
- Research four stocks in a similar category (for example, technology) and understand how the companies have progressed, why they vary, and why certain ones are succeeding more than others. Look at the dividends, the yields.
- Track a household budget.

The student in the following sample decided to track the household budget for her family. Following is one way to detail the project.

Sample Project

Problem: I am always hearing my parents complain about their expenses and that their cost of living is too high. It is affecting family dynamics and every decision made in the household.

Objective: To understand how the finances work in my home, and try to find solutions that are cost savings.

Audience: My family

Implementation: I created a detailed three-month analysis of the family expenses and I tracked them on a spreadsheet. I created a communications system that allows me to have access to my family's expenses and information, such as bills, expenses, receipts, entertainment, and so forth.

Obstacles/objections/competition: It was difficult to broach this subject with my parents. They seem to behave as if this is none of my business. After working with my mentor, I learned how to discuss money and respect their privacy, and try to be a contributor.

Result/impact: We instituted a new budget program that cut costs, and led to each family member taking on more responsibilities such as lawn mowing, housekeeping, laundering instead of dry cleaning, and cooking instead of eating out. We are now saving $700 per month.

My takeaways: I learned basic accounting skills, how to create an Excel spreadsheet, and how to create a budget and stick to it. I also learned how to talk to my parents about their finances. I learned how expensive the cost of living is and I learned some of the pressures my parents feel. I learned to be an active contributor in my home and that I make a difference. And, I have learned that I can work more in the summers.

Example 2

Class: sciences, technology, computers, IT

Possible mentor profession: engineer, IT professional, scientist, researcher, physicist, environmentalist

Project options:

- Environmental issue to be tested: research/test local bodies of water for pollutants.
- Create a new digital game that leaves the participants with a unique takeaway: lessons learned, new skills, uplifting messages.

- Research recycling: Do consumers understand how and why to recycle? How can the system be improved?
- Design a working app that fills an unmet need within your sphere of experience.

In the following sample, the student decided to design an app that would facilitate carpooling.

Sample Project

Problem: There are too many cars on the road, a lack of parking, and more driving leads to more pollution.

Objective: I created an interactive app for ride sharing that is good for up to thirty minutes before a ride is needed, thinking this would be particularly useful after school for students who don't drive.

Audience: I determined the audience being served; to start are parents with kids who don't drive or kids who don't have cars.

Implementation: The brand name for my app would be C-Pool. With my mentor, I have developed a branded logo, and will reach my audience through social media. The functional idea is for students needing a ride to log on, sharing their time and destination, and for student drivers or mothers to respond within a fifteen-minute grace period.

Obstacles/objections/competition: It has been difficult to find a timely method of marketing that reaches passengers and there are liabilities for putting under-age students together with adults. I know I need to discuss these obstacles with an attorney.

Result/impact: I tried a trial app with friends and parents in the neighborhood. It actually worked quite well amongst people that already knew each other. It was an easier way to communicate than having our moms all calling each other, and in the event of a no-show, emergency, or rain, it was faster to find transportation for all parties involved.

My takeaways: I learned that finding a linkage between strangers was challenging. I realized I would need to discuss this in depth with an attorney to determine what liabilities might be involved. Would I be liable if there were an accident? What would happen if a driver picked up a passenger who proved to be unscrupulous? As well, I have yet to figure out how to make this profitable, but perhaps if I made it a membership C-pool app that required background checks, I could turn a profit and protect both drivers and passengers.

Example 3

Class: art, graphic design, media, drama

Possible mentor professions: architect, graphic designer, advertising executive, film director or critic, musician, artist

Project options:

- Create a three-minute video selling an idea about which the student cares.
- Redesign graphically the student's favorite product or service in multiple media.
- Create a new jingle for a particular product or service.

In the following example, the student chose to redesign the graphics of a small neighborhood coffeehouse to attract more business.

Sample Project

Problem: Starbucks is so pervasive—I wanted to draw attention to a smaller yet competitive coffeehouse who also had outstanding coffees and teas.

Objective: My objective is to redesign the graphics and the physical space to draw a younger audience and create an expanded repeat customer base.

Audience: The audience I researched was coffee drinkers, from multiple age demographics and socioeconomic backgrounds, to better understand their purchasing decisions.

Implementation: I first studied competitive coffeehouses. I created a random questionnaire to learn why they selected a particular store, and what their profile was. Then I began to design newly enhanced products and graphics that would appeal to a new audience. Additionally, I studied the layout and flow of the store, based on complaints I heard from different target groups.

Obstacles/objections/competition: I was challenged by understanding the subjectivity of design, and the reactions of different audiences. This was an odd blend of art and business that I need to learn more about. I shifted visuals based on interview responses.

Result/impact: I presented to the store owner my research, new logo, enhanced product ideas, and graphics, explaining that I'm a student and that this was a guided mentor project for class. They were interested in my feedback and have begun to alter some of their menu items based on our conversations.

My takeaways: I learned that graphics and art are very subjective and that research is invaluable to gauge response. I'd like to learn much more about how to conduct deeper research and focus groups. I also learned it is very challenging to compete with a large institutional brand, but that doesn't mean we can't succeed. I enjoyed the creative process and having my ideas accepted and implemented. It was awesome!

Example 4

Class: social studies, English, journalism

Possible mentor professions: journalist, attorney, communications professional, lobbyist, politician, salesperson, administrator, manager, public relations professional

Project options:

- Select a community controversy or issue and raise awareness from a particular perspective.
- Urban sprawl results in too many deer being displaced. What are the options?

- What are the outcomes of so many school closings in our community?
- Is new real estate development contributing or detracting from our community experience?

The student decides to explore a community issue: the construction of a new shopping center.

Sample Project

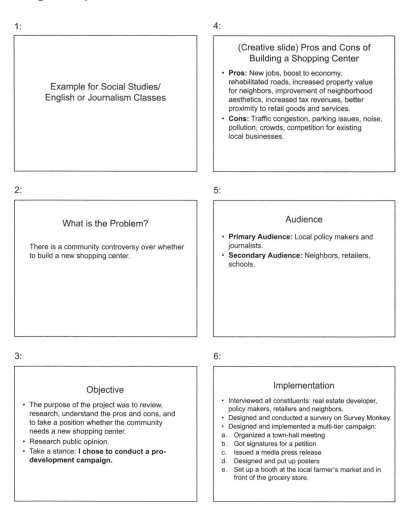

Figure 6.1 *PowerPoint Sample*

7:

Media Campaign

- Press release sent to 4 newspapers and 2 radio stations.
- Op-ed sent to 2 editorial boards.

8:

(Creative slide) Benefits of Shopping Center

- Projected tax revenue Increase of 15%.
- The project will be a mixed-use development: residential and commercial, thus providing new housing for the community.
- Parks and recreation areas will be included, as an added benefit to the community.
- Upgraded stores and restaurants.
- Provide needed retailers within walking distance.

9:

(Creative slide) Objections to Shopping Center and How to Overcome Them

Objections	Countering Objections
1. Increased traffic	1. Not all vehicle traffic, also foot traffic.
2. Parking problems	2. Garages will be built that can accommodate 200 cars.
3. Noise	3. Mixed use development includes heavy landscaping to abate noise and pollution. Stores will close by 8 pm and restaurants will be in the interior of the development.
4. Building heights	4. Developer assures there will only be three large stores.

10:

(Creative slide) Rendering of Shopping Center

11:

(Creative slide) Map of Traffic Patterns Showing Traffic Lights and Parking

12:

Results

- Three media outlets published articles or op-eds. Was interviewed by one radio station.
- I spoke to local groups such as the school PTA, citizen's association, and did public outreach.
- Received 2000 signatures on a petition, that showed the support of the local community.
- The city council voted to allow the development to proceed.

13:

My Take-Aways

- I learned about the relationships between community members, policy makers and the business community.
- I gained an understanding of how to conduct a grass-roots campaign.
- I envision myself employing these skills in politics or journalism in my future.
- Who knows, maybe I will run for office one day!

Figure 6.1 (*Continued*)

Recap

When embarking on this new mentoring adventure and building a collaborative relationship with the teacher, clearly establish your mutual goals from the beginning. Create a channel of communication, a feedback mechanism, and ongoing touch points of progress periodically.

As the school year unfolds, you will realize that you and the teacher are essentially teammates aligning to accomplish the same mission: your students' growth. You will be amazed by how much your mentees progress, how they take hold of an idea that is theirs and become charged, and how much confidence they gain. The students' successes particularly shine during their year-end presentations, thanks to all the one-on-one attention they received from you and the teacher throughout the year. At these moments, you can see how the skills gap really does begin to close.

CHAPTER 7

FIRST-DAY JITTERS

A Game Plan to Get You Started

I walk into each year's first class with a healthy balance of fear and excitement. Teens are brutally honest, spontaneous, unpredictable, and naturally skeptical of outsiders. They are also full of promise, creativity, and longing for opportunity. The challenge for me each year is to build trust. This can't happen quickly and it can't be forced.

—Philip McNeill, managing partner,
Farragut Capital Partners, veteran NFTE mentor

After being a mentor in class for more than fifteen years, I concur with the sentiment Phil McNeill offers in the epigraph to this chapter—mentoring still feels daunting yet exhilarating, every single first day that I enter a new classroom.

In your role as a mentor, the way you handle this first day and relate to students will help build trust and set the stage for the coming semester or year. The pointers and game plan outlined in this chapter will help your first day go smoothly. They have worked for me for years.

Create a Positive Atmosphere

To begin, you want to enter the classroom with the goal to create a positive atmosphere for the students. You are a new and friendly face they are curious to meet. They know you are coming, have heard about you, and, honestly, welcome someone who is *not* a teacher. Seek to make the classroom and individual mentoring environment one where you:

- Solicit ideas without judgment
- Listen and remain receptive to students' creativity
- Remain open, with an "almost anything goes" demeanor

These are all characteristics for which to strive. To help the students feel comfortable with you, encourage them to keep any class discussions among themselves and honor every individual's confidentiality. You promise to do the same.

Getting Geared Up

Like all first meetings—a job interview, a first date, your first day on the job—you may consider the matter of appropriate attire and the impression you will make on the students. A good rule of thumb is to strike a balance between coming across as someone representing the business world and someone who is "relatable" and a little cool.

Dress

It is fine to represent your occupation and dress the part. For example, if you typically wear a suit to work and are heading to the office afterward, wear a suit. However, be mindful not to create a chasm between you and the students because of your attire. "Business casual" is a good choice, but avoid flashy or intimidating jewelry or accessories.

Arrival

Be sure to arrive early to class. Some kids are welcoming and will eagerly introduce themselves. If they do not approach you first, introduce yourself and ask several students their names and something about themselves—their interests, favorite sports, or hobbies. During the class, refer to them by name. You will find that kids will connect with you more easily when you reference their peers and friends. Continue to connect with other students as they trickle into class.

Breaking the Ice

At this point, you have met the teacher and you saw the classroom during your pre-school meeting. The students have been informed you are coming; they are as excited to meet you as you are to meet them. The teacher will generally call everyone to order, make announcements, and then briefly introduce you.

Classes typically run between forty-five and ninety minutes, with fifteen to thirty students in a class. Keep these few tips in mind:

- In this high-tech era, attention spans have decreased. Your challenge is to keep the students' attention by changing your pace and tone frequently, telling short stories, and having fun.
- If you notice you are losing the students' attention, engage them in dialogue or ask questions such as these: "What would you do in this instance, Maryanne?" Or, "If you disagree with this idea, how would you propose to do it differently, George?"
- Speak to your audience at their level of understanding and don't get too technical. Bring in your personal experiences and speak with authenticity and emotion, saying things such as, "I took on this challenge and was fearful at first."

First-Day Action Plan

The following plan, a rough layout, provides some flexibility. It is meant to give you an agenda, as you may be accustomed to using in the business world. However, think of it as an "agenda lite"—that is, go with the flow, be flexible, and *listen* to what the students have to say. Make a one-on-one connection with each student.

Remember, your priority this first day is to break the ice, get the students to relate to you, and lay the first building block of a lasting relationship with your class.

Pick your preference regarding what you want to do and plan your time accordingly. Have the students write their names on a folded piece of paper displayed on their desks, or ask the teacher to have them prepare this before your arrival. Following is an example of how you might allocate your time, depending on the length of class:

1. Introduce yourself: explain why you are there and outline the plan for the day (five to ten minutes).
2. Play a class game as an icebreaker (up to twenty-five minutes).
3. Do student introductions: ask their names, grades, and project or business ideas (thirty to forty-five minutes).
4. Share your personal story: give an in-depth introduction (five to ten minutes—if time permits).

1. Introduce Yourself (Five to Ten Minutes)

Take a few minutes to explain *briefly* who you are and why you are there. During this welcome, you might weave a comment about the students you met earlier into your opening statement. Tell the class your name; the third-party organization you are with, if applicable (for example, NFTE, Youth Ventures, DECCA, Junior Achievement); and your connection with the organization, if applicable (for example, volunteer mentor, officer, member of the board of directors). Explain your role as a mentor, what students can expect from you, and how often you will be visiting the class (weekly, biweekly, monthly), and let them know that you look forward to working with them for the term, specifying whether it will be for a semester or a full year. If you are working with a collaborator or co-mentor, you can play off each other.

Explain how you will work with the students—one on one or in small groups. Establish some rules and expectations. If you plan to bring in guest speakers, let them know, but explain that *you* will be the main person visiting on a recurring basis. Ask the students if they have heard of your organization.

Lay out the plan for the day: explain that you will play a game, ask them to introduce themselves, and then spend more time telling them about yourself.

2. *Play Icebreaker Games (Up to Twenty-Five Minutes)*

Why is it important to play a game? I have discovered it is a tried-and-true way to break the ice, let the students see you as a real and animated person, and, most importantly, illustrate the principles that you hope to teach throughout the semester or year. This allows the students to let their guard down, to relax and ease into this new learning situation. Following, you will find a few examples of games I have used over the years.

Game 1: The $20 Game

This game teaches basic business, investments, and entrepreneurship; I made it into an experiential game and use it as my tried-and-true icebreaker.

Materials: a $20 bill and a piece of chalk or marker:

- Step 1. Question: "Who is good at giving a party?" Bring a volunteer to the front of the room and give that person a $20 bill. Ask Student A, "How will you use the $20 to put on a party?" Write his ideas on the chalkboard or smart board; for example, figure out where to host the party, buy sodas and snacks, ask a friend to DJ. The volunteer student then gives back the $20 and sits down.
- Step 2. Question: "Who is good at saving money?" Bring a volunteer to the front of the room and give that person the $20 bill. Ask Student B, "How will you save the money?" Write down her answer; for example, put it in the bank, put it under the mattress, and so forth. This volunteer also returns the $20.

- Step 3. Question: "Who is good at investing?" Student C comes up, takes the $20, and offers an idea about how to invest this money; for example, put it in a money market account or buy stocks or bonds. Then ask follow-up questions such as how much interest the investment will earn. This volunteer also returns the money.
- Step 4. Question: "Who is good at being an entrepreneur?" Student D comes to the front, takes the $20, and gives his answer. For example, he may say something like, "See this Hawaiian shirt I'm wearing? I bought it at the Dollar Store. I think I will resell these as my business." Ask members of the class what they would actually pay for a shirt like the one he is modeling. Students usually say about $7. Then say, "Do the math and determine the profit; for example, a profit of $6 per shirt would be $120." This student returns the $20.
- Step 5. Review what all of these volunteers did with the money:
  - Student A: "The party giver" spent the $20 on a party. He had a good time but has no money left.
  - Student B: "The saver" still has the same $20 she started with plus a small interest.
  - Student C: "The investor" either has less than she started with or potentially more, depending on the success of the chosen investment. Offer any of these real-life examples that show the potential profit or risk in the stock market:
    - In 1992, you could buy a share of Apple stock for $11.72. In December 2015, a share of Apple stock sold for approximately $114.
    - In 1992, McDonald's stock sold for $11.86 a share. In December 2015, a share cost about $116.
    - A share of Facebook stock sold for $38 when the stock went public in May 2012. That same day, it went up to $45, but in September 2012, it was selling for only $17.55 a share. In December 2015, it was selling for $103 a share.
  - Student D: "The entrepreneur" took a chance but earned a solid profit. The $120 profit can then be used to: have a party, save, invest, and *still* buy more shirts. Then tell the students, "*This* is what we are here to talk about!"

Table 7.1 $20 Game Results

	How They Spent the $20	*Result*
Student A	Threw a party	Had fun, $0 left
Student B	Saved it	Still has the same $20 with small interest added
Student C	Invested in stocks	Mixed: $10–$1,000+ after more than 20 years
Student D	Started a business	$120+ profit, can be used to throw a party, save, invest, and put back into the business!

Game 2: The Stand Up, Sit Down Game

This exercise gets the students thinking about business or project ideas. My friend and colleague Julie Kantor, president and CEO of Twomentor in Bethesda, Maryland, often used this fun game when she was a teacher. It gets kids on their feet and grabs their attention. It is versatile, so you can adjust to any subject matter: art, technology, science, and others.

Come up with a series of questions referring to your subject matter and ask the kids to stand up if they can answer yes to the question. Otherwise, they remain seated. A few sample questions for a mentor who is an expert in technology follow:

- Do you have more than twenty apps on your phone?
- Have you ever thought of an app you would like to develop?
- Have you ever written down your idea or explained it to a friend?

At the close of this game, the mentor can draw some conclusions as to how everyone is unique, we are all at differing stages of technology, how you enjoyed learning about the students' interests, and you will look forward to sharing your technology experience with them in the year to come.

Game 3: The Interview Game

The interview game allows the students to talk and connect with one another, become good listeners, and practice public speaking.

Ask the students to break into pairs, preferably with a student they do *not* know well, and to interview each other over a five-minute period using questions you have written on the board. Some ideas for questions include:

- What is your name?
- Where are you from?
- What is your native country or family's background?
- What are your talents and/or passions?
- What is something no one knows about you? Surprise us!
- What are your weaknesses/what are you afraid of?
- Where is an interesting place you have traveled?
- What is your favorite meal?
- If you had $1 million to give away, to whom would you give it?
- What is your favorite TV show?
- What concert would you choose to get front-row seats to see?
- Whom do you admire the most?

At the end of five minutes, select three or four students to stand and introduce the person they interviewed with a one-minute introduction; for a longer exercise, go around the whole class and listen to each person. This icebreaker works best with small groups, unless you have lots of time.

Game 4: Your Best You Game

This game fosters feelings of safety and openness as you help students get comfortable expressing themselves in front of others. Write the following on the board:

Name
Student year
What makes you happy?
What are your talents?
Are you praised often for these?
What are you passionate about?

Explain that we rarely think about these questions and actually talk about the answers aloud. We might fear it sounds like bragging, or that no one is interested. Tell the class: "But today, I (the mentor) care immensely about 'Your Best You.' As always, there is no right or wrong answer. I hope everyone will be respectful of each person's interests. I will start by sharing my own comments about myself: I know what makes me really happy in life is beautiful mountains, a sense of space, and music—absolutely all kinds of music. I wish I had more talent in music, but that is not the case. Over many years, however, I have learned I am good at connecting with people, I am trustworthy, and I am pretty good at marketing. Finally, I am passionate about my family, theater, and the arts. See, now you have learned quite a bit about me, and it is good to understand your own strengths and be able to vocalize them."

Now go around the room. As students share their self-perceptions, it is okay to comment on like interests or be supportive and enthusiastic. I also like to keep a running list with students' names and interests, so I can refer to this moment when we meet one on one.

Last, I find that kids are really happy after this exercise. Somehow, making these proclamations in front of the mentor, teacher, and classmates renders their ideas more real, and they become more connected because of this shared experience.

You are welcome to come up with your own game that either illustrates the field of study you represent or that you think would be a good icebreaker. (Please share this with us at www.teachtowork.com.)

3. *Student Introductions (Thirty to Forty-Five Minutes)*

During these introductions, you act as the facilitator for students sharing ideas, which is an ideal way to get to know the students better. Start by writing these three questions on the board, adjusting them if necessary to fit your field of study:

- Do you have an idea about a business you would like to start or a project you would like to do?

- Do you have a passion for something specific?
- Do you have a business you love to go to or a favorite product you like to buy or an issue that is weighing on your mind (relative to class subject)?

Like the tenet "hear and be heard," students listen more attentively *after* they have had an opportunity to share something about themselves. You might tell the students you are getting them into the practice of introducing themselves publicly. Interestingly, at Harvard Business School, students are instructed to never speak without standing up.

Next say, "Now, let's go around the room and let me hear your big ideas. *There are no right and wrong answers here.* Who wants to go first?" Don't be afraid to be casual and walk around the room while the students talk. To keep students on their toes and paying attention, you might bring a ball and toss it into the group. Whoever catches it goes next. Here are a few tips to keep in mind while the students make their introductions:

- Plan your time according to the number of students.
- Create a safe, positive environment for sharing and remind students to be creative and be themselves.
- Remind students that there are no right or wrong answers or bad ideas.
- How you receive each student as he shares is critical. You can take notes as students share ideas by writing down their names and ideas; this shows accountability and that you are paying attention and care about what they say.
- Interact with students about their ideas. One way is to make an affirmative or supportive statement such as, "That sounds really fascinating, Maria. How did you get interested in this?" Or challenge the student a bit and ask, "What will make your product different from what already exists, Dexter? Can you expand on that?" Or ask, "So, you want to start a bake shop, Layla. What will set your cupcakes apart from the rest on the market?"

- Get other students involved by asking them, "Would you buy this product?" or "How much would you pay for that?"
- Be animated and spontaneous. Make eye contact with the students as you focus on building good relationships with them.

4. Share Your Personal Story (Ten to Fifteen Minutes)

Your role as a mentor starts when you share your personal struggle—your own story about how you got to where you are on your career path. If you run out of time, you can tell your story at the beginning of your second visit.

Start by saying something like, "One of the reasons I am here with you is because of the difference [fill in the blank: business, technology, entrepreneurship, art] has made in my life." In my case, I would add, "I was not a wonderful student; studying was hard for me. It took a long time to find my stride and passion. I tried a lot of things. It was not until I was twenty-eight that I learned about business, and I found that was my spark. That is when I went for an A+ performance."

Be sure to say how much you enjoy your life in the business world. As you determine what you want to say, follow these tips:

- Start your story with a struggle the kids can relate to. Make your story personal or emotional. Share any fears or obstacles you encountered.
- Share your path, where you faltered or failed, and what you learned from each setback.
- How did you come up with your idea? Share why you love what you do.
- What are some of the challenges you face?
- How did you fund your business or product?
- How did you get your first customer?
- Share visuals or something tangible that pertains to your job—for example, architectural plans, photographs, or marketing materials.

Tom Brown, a former teacher at Anacostia High School in Washington, D.C., offers this advice: "Tell the students the worst experience you've had and how you resolved it. Then tell them the best one and what it meant to you."

You can close by conveying what has motivated many mentors to come back into the classroom year after year. Many have said, "I wish I'd had this kind of a class when I was your age. This is real world and can be life changing for you. The lessons you learn here will take you forward in anything you do."

Recap

Remember, calm first-day jitters as a mentor by being prepared. Recognize from the start that times have changed since you graduated, and today's schools contrast dramatically with those of yesteryear. Additionally, schools run quite differently from your business. Schedule changes, tardiness, and interruptions should be anticipated. Begin with an expectation of flexibility. Your goal from the beginning will be to create a positive atmosphere in which students feel comfortable exchanging ideas, assured there is no such thing as a right or wrong concept. Play some tried-and-true icebreaker games to begin to get to know the kids and to give them an opportunity to begin to know you. Be relaxed, open, and personable, and the students will follow your lead.

CHAPTER 8

ONE ON ONE

Building Rapport, One Student at a Time

People who grew up in difficult circumstances and yet are successful have one thing in common . . . at a critical junction in their early adolescence they had a positive relationship with a caring adult.

—President William Jefferson Clinton

Beginning a one-on-one, cross-generational dialogue is easy for some but daunting for others. The very act of showing up, caring, and giving your knowledge, however, has an enormous residual effect for each and every student fortunate enough to have a mentor like you. This chapter is designed to reinforce your rapport as you embark on this adult–adolescent encounter.

In Thomas Friedman's September 10, 2014, *New York Times* article, "It Takes a Mentor," he pointed to results from recent Gallup research on education practices that measured students' long-term success in the workplace after leaving school. The study confirmed conclusively that college graduates were more predisposed to "overall well-being" in life and productivity in the workplace if, while they were in school, they had an adult (professor or mentor) who nurtured them as a person or who encouraged their ideas.[1]

This chapter will identify the elemental steps of creating an open, positive dialogue between mentor and mentee. Additionally, it will explore ways you can help your mentee through some of her learning obstacles. It will paint a picture of students' challenges so you will be better equipped to relate to and understand them. I will share some of my own practical knowledge of working with adolescents for more than twenty years, fifteen as a mentor and five before that as a counselor for incarcerated youth. I will also draw from recent research on learning psychology.

What We Are, What We Are Not

It is important to note the distinction between our role as business professionals, who are there to lend guidance and motivation around a student project, and that of emotional health counselors, who guide teens through life's problems. For example, your golf coach is there to help you develop a golf swing, not to hear about your marital problems. Although we may at times be working with vulnerable youth, and need to understand the different dynamics, our role is that of a supportive coach helping the students toward completion of an assignment. Studies show that youth relate more easily through a shared activity and events than through dialogue alone. Last, completion of a project can and does build students' self-esteem. It can take them away from self-pity or spiraling negativity. To these ends, your intergenerational connection can well serve youth in more ways than you can imagine.

Understanding Youth and Risk Factors

We were all young once, but today's youth are different for many reasons. For one thing, they now have proliferating social media, the Internet, and access to hours of unfiltered information. Social scientists and behaviorists are busy calculating the emotional effects on youth and their relationships to automation versus to humans, as groundbreaking social phenomena. Indeed, this is only one of the factors contributing to changes in adolescence, particularly from the time when we, as mentors, were teens.

Experts report that a student's socioeconomic background can be a predictor of his future. In Robert D. Putnam's recent book, *Our Kids: The*

American Dream in Crisis, he discusses an *inequity of opportunity.* While poor kids may have few mentors, lack people in their lives they can trust, participate in fewer sports or after-school activities, and have limited exposure to networks, he suggests that students from wealthier backgrounds not only have far more options but have adults in their lives who help steer them away from negative influences.

Faced with an onslaught of pressures, many youth cannot escape the risk factors that infiltrate their school, community, and home environments, such as:

School

- Peer pressure, including gangs
- Substance abuse
- High dropout rates
- Negative values
- Cyberbullying
- Inconsistent discipline
- Lack of one-on-one attention

Neighborhood

- Neighborhood violence
- Lack of supervision
- Teenage pregnancy
- Gang threats
- Lack of adult role models

Home

- Single or preoccupied parent(s)
- Stress
- Lack of discipline, little structure
- Financial difficulties
- Limited supervised time, limited quality time with parents

- Poor nutrition
- Abuse and violence
- Lack of security, frequent moves, moving and rotating adults
- Disorderly environment

There are simply not enough positive adult figures in the lives of many youth who desperately need them. Our national history has been threatened with socio-economic gaps before, and underlying our responses then, Putnam suggests, was a value system in which "there was a commitment to invest in other people's children—a deeper sense that those kids—were our kids."[2] Putnam highlights that one of the potential ways to diminish the growing opportunity gap today, as before, is if *more* people take on this mentorship role with ownership that "America's poor belongs to us and we to them." As, Jay Ash, city manager of Chelsea (a suburb of Boston), told the *Boston Globe*, "If our kids are in trouble, my kids, our kids, anyone's kids, we all have a responsibility to look after them."[3]

Often, out of a sense of survival, many urban youth have learned to be independent and responsible. A fight-or-flight mode becomes embedded. They may have to look after their younger siblings. They may have to prepare meals and clean the house. They may have to hold down a job or two to help contribute to household expenses. But if we delve a little deeper, we begin to understand that these teens' emotional needs are not nurtured.

While they may survive day by day, they often lack fundamental support or adult attention that is focused on them and their well-being. No one is listening to them, asking how they feel or how their day was, or spending quality time during non-school hours. In *Our Kids,* Putnam describes two sisters, Sofia and Lola, teens from Orange County's working class, who, when asked about their rule of thumb, their moral compass, replied, "You can't trust anyone, not even your best friends."[4]

As a result of the pressures young people face, they commonly experience a lack of self-esteem, suffer from depression, experience suicidal thoughts, or have a feeling of disenfranchisement. This scenario can easily lead to societal danger—one lost, misdirected youth at a time—starting with a kid dropping out of school, followed by an enticement of criminal activity for easy money, or potentially a new allegiance to an extremist sect that supply youth with a sense of belonging. These youth build a sense of mistrust as a means to guard against more pain and disappointment. Many lack the time, inclination, or role models to even consider their future or aspirational goals, particularly when they are just trying to survive.

"The idea that so many children are born into poverty in the wealthiest nation on Earth is heartbreaking enough," said President Barack Obama. "But the idea that a child may never be able to escape that poverty because she lacks a decent education . . . or a community that views her future as their own . . . that should offend us all."[5]

I spell out this background so you will be aware of the unknowns that could be affecting our student population. As mentors, we are but one touch point on these kids' path to adulthood; we are ambassadors to another world and the potential it holds. Your attention, particularly in this one-on-one scenario, can be critical to each and every child you encounter.

The Learning Mindset

I have painted a broad-brush view of the potential risks students you meet might be facing. Couple those with self-esteem issues and limited foundational support, and you begin to understand why learning and motivation can be difficult. Of course, all of these influences affect our role as mentors, and it is valuable to revisit some of the newest concepts from experts.

One of my favorite sources, which has helped me in my own life and as a mentor, is the research of Carol Dweck, the renowned Stanford University psychologist. I had the opportunity to hear her speak at the Aspen Ideas Festival in 2013 and an opportunity to interview her recently. I have never forgotten her talk. She suggested that, whether students are aware of it or not, they are terrible at estimating their own abilities, and that the immense power to *believe in oneself* can strongly affect a person's desire to learn, her overarching achievement, and her life's potential.

Dweck's talk posed for me a core question about myself and my own learning. I have even posed this question to dinner guests and debated it with fellow mentors—I ask you to consider your own response as well: *Which came first for you, your confidence or your success?* This brings up questions such as, how do we first begin to believe in ourselves? Where do we find the grit or stamina to barrel through difficulty? And how do we teach others to achieve?

Dweck's opening comment in 2013 created for me an internal dialogue that has led to my own observations of my work as a mentor. I sat on the edge of my seat throughout her talk. It was as if I was hearing the psychology of my own learning. She stimulated those old insecure feelings of being in school, the uncertainty of not knowing if I could succeed, and the fear of trying. Hmm, what created that? And when did it go away? What was my attitude toward encountering new information both publicly and privately in the past? And how has it changed?

Dweck wrote about her landmark research in her book *Mindset: The New Psychology of Success*. When we spoke, she shared that she had always been interested in researching people's learning patterns and why some avidly avoid challenges while others relish the difficulty brought by obstacles. Some of her research included the study of young children who were given extremely challenging puzzles to assemble. She observed their responses to gradations of difficulty and levels of effort, and concluded that some children walked away feeling like a failure and just stopped trying. Conversely, others were persistent, remained challenged, and relished the struggle of conquering the puzzle. After years of research, Dweck developed her learning theory about mindsets, calling one a "fixed mindset" and the other a "growth mindset"—terms that have become well known in the field of education, sports, and business management. I have included these descriptions to help you better understand the learning characteristics of students you might meet. Following is a brief overview of the two mindsets, derived from both her Aspen talk and from a graph in the back of her book, *Mindset*.

A **fixed mindset** is characterized by a desire to look smart. Responses might include:

> *Challenges*: Avoid
>
> *Obstacles*: Get defensive or give up early
>
> *Effort*: See effort as fruitless or worse
>
> *Criticism*: Ignore useful or negative feedback
>
> *Success of others*: Feel threatened by others' success[6]
>
> *Intelligence*: Something you are born with that can't be changed; "that's that"
>
> *Qualities*: Fixed and "carved in stone"
>
> *Importance*: Gained by "proving yourself"
>
> *Values*: Based on success or failure (for example, look smart, not dumb; be accepted not rejected; be a winner not a loser)
>
> *School:* Only participates if certain of the right answer
>
> *Relationship*: Chooses a partner who bolsters his/her ego

As a result of these responses, the person with a fixed mindset may plateau early and achieve less than his full potential.

A **growth mindset**, on the other hand, is characterized by a desire to learn. Responses might include:

> *Challenges*: Embraced
>
> *Obstacles*: Persist in the face of setbacks
>
> *Effort*: Path to mastery
>
> *Criticism*: Learn from
>
> *Success of others*: Find lessons and inspiration in others' success
>
> *Intelligence*: No matter how much one has been given, she can always change and grow
>
> *Qualities:* Passion for stretching one's self, sticking with something especially when things are not going well
>
> *Importance*: Sets high standards, seeks feedback, and develops through "process"

Values: Come from risk, confronting challenge, working until something is figured out

School: One is here to learn

Relationship: Chooses a partner who can challenge him/her, leading to growth

The person with a growth mindset, as a result of his responses, can reach ever higher levels of achievement.

By understanding the two mindsets, we learn that we have a *choice*. Which do we want to inhabit? The growth mindset is learned, and as mentors this list of characteristics is valuable to help a mentee begin to understand that learning is an attitude, a decision. In addition, this list can help you identify some of your mentee's characteristics.

Overcoming Doubt

I realized as Dweck spoke that many of her ideas for working through students' challenges resonated with my own experience as a mentor. The attitudes were also familiar to me from learning how to play a sport or an instrument. How do you mentor someone through an obstacle and help him conquer self-doubt? Following are some ideas gleaned from my experience and from talking to teachers, coaches, and authors.

Rein in Self-Judgment

A teen might fall into a spiral of negative thinking: an "I'm so stupid" feeling can take over, and his self-talk can be brutal and impede efforts. You, as mentor, can help by having the student focus on the facts. If he has had a bad outcome, help him collect evidence. Discuss all the ways that the student *is* competent, and even list them. The goal is to stop the "I'm so stupid" conversation and look objectively at the hard cumulative facts. Hopefully this will help the student overcome these self imposed obstacles.

Praise the Process

Dweck emphasized what she called "process praise." The idea is to make *effort* a priority. She recommends always tying praise to something the student did. It can be counterproductive to compliment an innate talent, physical attribute, or skill. Instead, say something such as:

> What did you learn today?
> What did you try hard at?
> What are you struggling with?

Project Based Mentoring focuses on progress discussions. Ask questions such as: What steps have you taken? What are your obstacles? What are your strategies for overcoming them? And remember to praise the effort, the strategy, and the execution.

Encourage a Concrete Plan

I was recently in class in Florida with a fellow mentor, Stuart Halpert, who stood in front of the class and said, "You know how I get things done? Every day I make a list. I know it won't get done if I don't write it down and make a plan." He even pulled out his iPhone and read aloud "Today's List." He shared his workout regimen, his daily call to his kids, his household assignments, and steps for his investment projects. The idea is to help a student design tangible steps toward her goal.

Dr. Peter Gollwitzer, a New York University psychologist who studies people and tasks, suggests that people who talk about "getting things done tomorrow" rarely ever do. Asking "what, when, how, and where?" lead to high levels of follow-through. These questions also assist the task doer in visualizing how something will get done.

Teach Time Management

Time management is often daunting for students. Sometimes I pull out a pencil and paper and draw a calendar. Together with a student, we pencil in his fixed schedule versus his free time. We might discuss how long he thinks it will take to accomplish the first step of a task. Breaking projects down incrementally, step by step, is often the answer to accomplishing a goal that can otherwise seem insurmountable.

Highlight Mindset Choice

"To be average, to be labeled dumb," Dweck writes in *MindSet*, "is not a static way of life. A student might look turned off, but I saw that they never stop caring. Nobody gets used to feeling dumb."[7] The message we, as mentors, can offer, Dweck suggests is, "*You are in charge* of *your learning and your mindset.* It's a choice." This is an important message to convey repeatedly.

I believe part of our role as mentors is to guide students through a learning and, therefore, a growth experience and help them achieve a difficult accomplishment. Students who've achieved a goal take pride in the success of completion and learn that the process can recur through life. I've also seen that, as a result of this process, a student's self-narrative can begin to shift.

Empathetic Listening

What are some inroads to building rapport with a mentee? It is critical for you, as a mentor, to grasp the concept of empathy. The word is defined by the *American Heritage Dictionary* as "Understanding so intimate that the feelings, thoughts, and motives of one are readily comprehended by another" (after the Greek word *empatheia,* passion).[8] As a mentor, you must step out of your own life—bounded by your upbringing, your career, your family—and try to understand the perspective and experience of your mentee.

Learning to listen includes observing more than the words the person conveys. Much that is communicated isn't verbal—when an individual is not talking, he is still behaving in some manner. "One of the most important skills of effective listening is listening to nonverbals," said Madelyn Burley-Allen in her book *Listening: The Forgotten Skill.*[9]

Empathy is *the art of letting the speaker know* you not only understand the ideas spoken but are sensitive to the feeling that is being expressed. Psychologists are particularly good at this, because they are so removed emotionally from the subject and the information. They have learned to listen to the subtleties of expression. They are adept at being a mirror for the speaker, offering responses like, "You sound excited about your progress," "What's got you down today, your voice doesn't have the same bounce?" or "What I'm really hearing you say is . . ." They have responded not to a topic but to a feeling or a nonverbal signal.

According to James J. Deary III, at the Institute for Urban Family Health in New York City, "When two speakers begin to listen with the same enthusiasm with which they speak and to convey to one another that they heard both *what was said and how it was said,* a powerful bond begins to develop."

An Exercise for You, the Mentor

Before reading further, please take a moment and complete the Seven Principles of Trust Game, below. You will discover this game takes you to a vulnerable place and raises several questions, such as:

- Who gets you? Who is empathetic to your circumstances?
- How have people shown their true characteristics to you?
- What is the quality of relationships in your life?
- What is trust? How is it conveyed?
- Who is really there for us during our difficult times?

The Seven Principles of Trust Game

To play:

- On the top line of a piece of paper set up like the game card below, write the names of seven people who are important to you in your life.
- Score each person on each characteristic. A range of five scores is used for the grades: 1, 1.5, 2, 2.5, or 3. One is the lowest; 3 is the highest.
- Add up each individual's score. The highest possible score is 21.
- Next, add all the scores together. Divide the overall total by 7 (or the number of people listed).
- The result is a gauge of the amount of trust in your life, with 21 representing a perfect score.

NAMES   _____   _____   _____   _____   _____   _____   _____

EMPATHY
CARE
CAPABLE
WISDOM
PERMANENCE
TOTALITY
GENEROSITY

SUBTOTALS   _____   _____   _____   _____   _____   _____   _____
GROUP TOTAL   _____
DIVIDE BY NUMBER OF INDIVIDUALS   _____

As adults, we have experience on our side. We are toughened, have deep support systems, and can rely on coping mechanisms that we have developed over time. The teens you will be working with will not necessarily have this full arsenal.

I am *not* suggesting you ask these questions of your students, and in fact I suggest that you *do not*. But pause for a minute to think about who exemplifies these characteristics for you; how do you learn whether or not you can trust someone? This exercise is designed to evoke more empathetic behavior in you rather than spark a conversation with others.

Now, try to imagine you are fifteen years old. Your mentee might come from a compromised background, may have a single parent who works three jobs— she may not have *anyone* who takes an interest in her day to day, and though she seems tough she might experience neglect or loneliness. Who does she turn to for wisdom, empathy, caring, or permanence? Where does she learn about trust?

As you embark on building this new one-on-one relationship, you can turn to the ideas, role-playing games, and sample conversations that follow to help you create a safe space for the students you work with, in the hope that you will embody some of these seven principles of trust for your mentees. Please consider how trust has been shown to you in your adult life, and be creative and patient.

Establishing a One-on-One Dialogue

I have used the following set of scripts and questions, divided by topic, for the last fifteen years with great success. These points are designed as a reference to take you through a student project, or to enhance or stimulate your conversations with a young person in a nonjudgmental and supportive way. The questions assume that the mentor has already shared his background and professional experience with the class (see chapter 9, where I discuss leading the class). These questions help me begin building a relationship with the students I mentor. I use the name "Jack" below to refer to a hypothetical student and I start by telling Jack I would like us to mutually agree on some ground rules before we get started.

Authority

- Before we begin, Jack, I want to ask, *who is the biggest authority person in your life now?* (Maybe he answers "Mom.") What does authority mean to you?

- Have you ever heard the term consultant? Do you know what a consultant is?
- Well, I want you to know, Jack, that I am not your (Mom or the other authority figure named), I am more like your consultant. What that means is, *you are the boss.* You can accept or reject my suggestions, because this is *your* project. What I bring to bear is experience, ideas, and support. We can brainstorm, but *the ultimate decisions here are yours.* Are you cool with that?

Safe Space

- *Have you ever been in a place where there are no wrong answers? Where you can be completely creative? Where you can ask anything you want, anytime?*
- Welcome to our own safe space. This is where we get to think out loud. There are no limits on ideas. We are brainstorming. You can bounce any ideas off me, and vice versa, and we can talk about them. *Does that make sense to you? Do you have any thoughts or questions on how this will work?*
- Our safe space is kind of a new dynamic that is actually *fun*! We can break down the walls and think outside the box—you know, test hypothetical questions against logic, strategize, and see what sticks.

Confidentiality

- The last ground rule is that *anything you say, as relates to our project, is confidential*—I, potentially, will share an overview progress report with the teacher, but I will run this by you first. What does that mean? You don't have to worry that your ideas will leave this room. You can trust that our project conversations will remain between us. *Note for mentors: Confidentiality is important, but if you, as a mentor, ever come to understand that there is a threat of suicide, abuse, or possible harm to the student, you have an obligation to disclose this to the teacher or the nonprofit that has placed you in your mentor role.*

Identifying a Project

- So, Jack, let's start by sharing your ideas. What are you thinking about for your project?
- Would you share with me where this idea comes from? Why is it important to you? What prompted you to go down this road?
- Who is your audience? Who will your project serve? What is the age group or socioeconomic background of your audience? Where do they live geographically? What are their interests?
- Describe how you are thinking of carrying out the project. What steps do you foresee? What do you anticipate the outcome will be? What real-world impact do you envision?
- On a scale of one to ten, how excited are you about the project? I am asking because we will be working on this for quite a while, a semester or a year. You should be enthusiastic about it and it should hold your interest.

Rethinking Project Scope

- Jack, I want to ask, how is this project meaningful to you and why? It is more important for you to find a project that is meaningful to you, one that taps into your interests and your skill set, than to simply find a project. Later on, it can be tweaked or adjusted, but at the outset it is really good to have a framework from which to expand. I will ask you a few trigger questions that might help you think about your project scope and allow me to help you better identify other options.
- Jack, at (insert his age), your interests and priorities begin to shift. Maybe they've even changed from a few years ago. Most important, you are unique, with a whole set of skills, interests, and talents that

are uniquely yours. As you grow, you begin to learn more and more about yourself. So, here are a few questions that might help us both better know who you are.

- What kinds of things do you do that make you really happy?
- Which activities do you enjoy the most?
- What activities do you shy away from or dislike?
- What are your biggest fears with this project?
- What particular talent have you been praised for? What are your strengths?
- Is there a craft that you love?
- What projects do you do around the house?
- Name two role models you particularly respect.

Note for mentor: these questions might shift based on the scope of the project or the subject of your class. In an entrepreneurship class, for example, we would ask students questions about their skills, which could help determine their service or product. Other projects might make use of students' strong interpersonal or research skills, experience conducting interviews or crunching data, or adeptness with technology.

- Now that you have considered some focusing questions, Jack, let's discuss options for your project that you would really enjoy, and once you've found a project that is a good fit for you, we can start writing a first draft of the project objective.

Action Plan

- It helps to outline a flow chart for the project. Why don't we start with a due date and work backwards? I know this is hypothetical, but let's talk about the end game first.
- How long do you think it would take to prepare your final presentation, including all the elements of a PowerPoint presentation? How long might it take for the letters, research, photos, interviews, and so forth necessary to complete the project? How much time should we

leave for preparation for the final presentation? (Usually, two months is a good time frame.)

- Working backward allows us to determine how many months will be needed to do the bulk of the project research and discovery.
- Let's block out a calendar and determine a time frame for each phase together.
- Let's go through, step by step, how you want to execute your project and determine if the time frame is realistic.

Note for mentor: it takes organization to keep large projects on track. Students often need help with this. I might even purchase a three-ring binder with tabs to help track progress and ask the student to bring it to each meeting.

Check-In Updates

- "Jack, it's been ten days since we met, and my notes say we left off with your detailed action plan that included x-y-z. I'm really interested to hear what has happened, and our progress to date."
- "Jack, what were some of the issues you were facing this week with your progress? What were your triumphs, and what were your struggles? Let's talk about them."
- "It's important for you to know, Jack, that this is your schedule, and your action plan, so let's base these steps on what you can realistically accomplish. Please feel free to use me as a sounding board and if you want we can look at your schedule together."

Note for mentor: each meeting a student might leave with a student-directed action plan. It's critical that the student creates, writes, and buys into his next three or four steps. We each get a copy and at each meeting resume where we left off. In my experience, when the student sees me taking notes during each visit, in a subliminal way, it signals accountability because he knows that I know and that I care. Additionally, it keeps us on track, prevents us from wasting time, and we can pick up right where we left off. It's like we mean business and are teaching business behavior!

- If a student is stuck, you might say, "Jack, tell me about the best parts of your project that you've worked on recently. Tell me about what you are excited about now."

  Have him start with what is most interesting about the project in its current state. Later, go back to other, more difficult pieces.

  Or, have your mentees talk to you about their ideas for moving forward. "Jack, describe for me your next steps as you see them. What is the big picture, moving forward?"

  As the student speaks, write his concepts on your paper, taking notes until he is finished. Then read his ideas back to him. "This is what I heard you saying. Is this correct?" Sometimes the student is more creative aloud with you than he is by himself.

- Share your own story of overcoming an obstacle that is similar. "Jack, you know you are not the only one that has experienced obstacles. I remember a project I had to tackle and what I had to do to get through . . ."

- Work through steps aloud, and write an incremental action plan that you and the student mutually determine. "Jack, tell me what you think the next steps should be, and lets go from there . . ."

- Role-play: When your mentee doesn't know how to tackle an interview, or set up an appointment, you might role play like this: "Jack, if it were me, I would set up the interview with this kind of dialogue, keeping in mind what you are trying to accomplish, and being respectful and to the point . . . Remember, this person is busy, and would have to be making time for you. An example might sound like this . . ."

Note for mentor: you might role play as Jack, and let Jack role play as the interview subject. Possibly discuss some empathetic listening, to help Jack better understand his subject's viewpoint, time limits, or priorities—this way he can learn through you a new interpretation of how he might sound or a new method of dialogue. Then it can be productive to switch places and let

Jack frame the dialogue in his own words as you become as the interview subject.

Affirmation

"Jack, I remember when we started this project, do you? Do you remember the vision we discussed, the projection? It's fascinating to see where we've come, how far, and where it's all heading . . ." Or, "Jack, you have tackled, step by step, big questions set forth by this project . . . I'm really proud of you and can't wait to see what's next."

Note for mentor: students are usually unaccustomed to long-term projects, so they need to hear that they are making progress and be reminded of how far they have come. Keep in mind the suggestion to praise on *process, effort, strategy,* and *choice* rather than praising an innate ability, talent, or skill. Robert Sternberg, a psychologist and author of *Successful Intelligence,* suggests that a major factor in whether people achieve expertise is not some fixed prior ability but purposeful engagement. The following encouraging comments also, might help your mentee:

- I am so proud of you—you have really come far in your efforts.
- I can tell you've put work into this project; it is impressive.
- I believe you are going to have an impactful presentation that will be competitive. Keep up the good work.
- Jack, you have exceeded all expectations. This is awesome! What are your takeaways so far? What have you learned?

Research

Spend time discussing research with your mentee to be sure he is on the right track. Ask:

- Jack, what are your research findings?
- Tell me, do they vary from your expectation? If so, tell me how.

- Let's discuss your next steps? Do you want to talk about other resources and how to reach them?

Overview

- Jack, in the big picture, how do you feel we are progressing against our overview schedule?
- Are you pleased, excited, frustrated with our progress?
- What are your current needs? Would you like to change anything, based on what we now know?
- How can I help you?
- How will your findings to date fit with the overall assignment in terms of objective, implementation, result, or takeaway?

Improving Your Listening Skills

A study by Dr. Ralph Nichols suggests that we devote 40 percent of our day to listening, yet tests revealed that people listen at only 25 percent efficiency, according to Madelyn Burley-Allen's *Listening: The Forgotten Skill.*[10] With effort and self-training, we can improve our listening skills by using the following nine responses, which are particularly applicable in an intergenerational dialogue where language skills can be disparate. These were paraphrased from the section of Allen's book called, "The Art of Asking Questions."[11]

1. **Clarify unfamiliar phrases.** When a mentee speaks in vernacular you don't understand, feel free to say so. Or repeat the phrase and say, "Can you explain this in a different way?"
2. **Encourage without bias.** If the mentee stops talking, or you sense discomfort—you might repeat where she left off gently, and see if she will resume. Empathy is more important than opinion or bias.

3. **Refocus digressions.** When the speaker goes off on a tangent, you might keep her focused by saying, "I think you were about to explain . . ."

4. **Summarize points.** If you experience a mentee saying the same thing repeatedly, you might intervene and summarize with points a, b, and c, which demonstrates that you've heard, and you can then ask if you've missed anything.

5. **Clarify positions.** If a mentee contradicts himself, do not hesitate to ask him to clarify his statement, and ask how that weighs against an earlier statement. Your listening and asking is helping him clarify a position that might be contradictory.

6. **Restate opinions.** When you sense a student has strong opinions, it is helpful to repeat those opinions back and paraphrase them. This allows your mentee to know you have heard her, and it helps to hear her idea in another's voice.

7. **Respond to signs of nonverbal disagreement.** When you notice a distinct body language or facial expression change, you might go ahead and comment on it. "Is something bothering you? What just happened that made you respond that way? I want to understand."

8. **Clarify resistance.** When your mentee disagrees verbally, you might say something like, "What about that idea is flawed to you? Are there portions that are correct? How would you suggest we change the wording or the idea to better reflect your thoughts?"

9. **Ask for specifics.** Often, kids will speak in generalities, so try to pin them down for everyone's understanding. Ask, "What examples specifically explain that idea?" Or, "Do you have a story you can share that will clarify this for me?"

Communication Guidelines

As mentors, we cannot fix students' problems. We can, however, be kind, patient, supportive, and reliable in order to help them accomplish a task. I have compiled this list after talking with educators, adolescent therapists, nonprofit leaders, and teen mentors. Please keep these hints in mind as you work with students one on one.

- Make your communication positive.
- Listen without interrupting.
- Facilitate in a way that fosters the student's *own* ideas.
- Show up on time; be reliable.
- Listen for feelings and emotion, as well as words.
- Meet the students where they are emotionally.
- Be patient, without exception.
- Recognize and respect that the mentee may have a different point of view.
- Stand by your students shoulder to shoulder. Meet them at their level.
- Remember, adults tend to relate to one another more verbally. Youth relate more through activities or project based learning.
- Don't lecture or preach.
- Put aside your needs.
- Demonstrate interest with active listening.
- Keep it simple.
- Be genuine, real, and honest.
- Create comfort, even in failure.
- Show your belief that the student *can* succeed.
- Build self-esteem by praising effort, not talent.
- Don't be quick to give answers—instead, encourage the student to be resourceful.

Recap

In the end, listening is a way of saying to the speaker, "You are important." By listening, you are increasing the speaker's self-esteem. Everyone has a basic need for recognition. By giving someone your attention, you imply that you **respect** and **value** what she thinks. What a gift you are giving these students!

Notes

1. Thomas Friedman, "It Takes a Mentor," *New York Times*, September 9, 2014.
2. Robert D. Putnam, *Our Kids: The American Dream in Crisis* (New York: Simon & Schuster, 2015), 261.
3. Yvonne Abraham, "Doing Right by the Children in Chelsea," *Boston Globe*, August 31, 2014, accessed March 27, 2016, https://www.bostonglobe.com/metro/2014/08/30/doing-right-children-chelsea/mMQi2RET1PuVzXAwSrySOM/story.html.
4. Putnam, *Our Kids*, 150.
5. Barack Obama, "Remarks by the President on Economic Mobility" (speech at THEARC, Washington, DC, December 4, 2013), accessed February 3, 2016, https://www.whitehouse.gov/the-press-office/2013/12/04/remarks-president-economic-mobility.
6. Carol Dweck, *Mindset: The New Psychology of Success* (New York: Ballantine Books, 2007), 245.
7. Dweck, *Mindset*, 219.
8. *The American Heritage Dictionary*, 1973 edition (fourth), s.v. "empathy."
9. Madelyn Burley-Allen, *Listening: The Forgotten Skill* (New York: John Wiley & Sons, 1995), 56.
10. Burley-Allen, *Listening*, 96.
11. Burley-Allen, *Listening*, 123.

CHAPTER 9

LESSON PLANS FOR LEADING THE CLASS

The World through Your Lens

Kevin Burke (CEO of Centuria) has gone into several classrooms in the D.C. area to tell at-risk kids his story. In the process of doing so, he's uncovered a gem: helping kids like himself heals his soul.[1]

—Steve Mariotti, founder of Network for
Teaching Entrepreneurship (NFTE)

When you mentor, you will be bringing the outside world and new perspectives to students. You will enable them to learn about new milieus in a variety of ways:

- When you **work side by side** with your mentees on their projects on a recurring basis, students will experience emotional support, participate in a collaborative process, and develop the fortitude to finish.
- When you **lead the class** and share your journey, and when you conduct case studies in your area of expertise, students will begin to understand an industry from your vantage point.
- When you bring in **guest speakers** who describe their unique role and purpose, students will perceive a new outlook on the professional world.

- When you take students on **field trips** to explore and research their projects, they will begin to learn new knowledge with application to the professional world.

Through all these interactive experiences, you expose students, both physically and emotionally, to a new world of possibility. If I were to summarize the depth of the emotional gains expressed by students over the years in the thousands of letters they have sent me, I would say to mentors:

- You stimulate curiosity in students simply by showing up.
- Anecdotes about your pathway, complete with obstacles overcome, often trigger a new inner dialogue for students, who think, "If she did this, then I can too." You are planting a significant seed for motivation and engagement.
- When you advance to explaining skills and actionable events, you enlighten students about *how* to accomplish a goal. Your willingness to be there, to guide them through their own discovery, to assist them in a difficult process, and to inspire them to try something new is teaching them to be resourceful, even when it's hard.
- Last, you introduce students to a new, professional world, with industry-related speakers, tangible field trips, and what it means to be accountable in terms of research and data. This transformative combination opens a new world of *possibility*.

Bringing New Worlds to Class

What's amazing about mentorship as part of education is students begin to emulate you. You are an ambassador of achievement. An emissary of 'how to' in the real world. By showing up on a recurring basis, over time, they begin to perceive themselves as part of this previously unattainable world that you have made accessible. This makes all the difference.

Let's delve into some specifics about different roles you can play in leading the class.

Leading a Class: Your Expertise

Planning a fifty- to ninety-minute class based on your expertise, simplified for a young audience, can be an exhilarating yet intimidating experience. It can be challenging to make the lesson relevant, experiential, and fun enough to hold the attention of a classroom full of students. It definitely gives you a new appreciation for what teachers do every day.

Following, find examples that can be adapted for different types of classes and subject matters. Discuss your scope and class design with the teacher in advance to be certain it fits into the curriculum.

The Case Method

The case method, developed at the Harvard Business School, is used in a variety of universities, including the Harvard Business School, Yale School of Management, University of Virginia Darden School of Business, and the Marine Corps University. This teaching approach exposes students to world issues—principles, analysis, and problem solving—by using "decision-forcing cases," or decision games that ask students to take on the role of a person faced with a dilemma.

What sets the case method apart from other approaches is that the instructor refrains from providing his own opinions and instead asks students to devise and defend their own solutions to problems.

This is how it works: the leader—in this case you—presents a narrative or overview about an individual (or individuals) who is embroiled in a challenging problem, and then stops the story at the point where a decision needs to be made. The students are then asked to analyze the case from all angles, discuss the problem with those in their study group to get more perspectives, and devise their own solutions. The instructor prepares discussion points, takeaways, and questions to lead the conversation.

A particular case can fill a class, or may be extended over several classes, and the method can incorporate role-playing, debates, and deep discussion of the dilemma. In some classes where I have used this method, my co-mentor and I have invited a guest speaker to present his story up to a pivotal crossroad for his business. Then we pause. Students break out into four or five groups with assignments and make recommendations to the guest speaker for what he might do next. After listening to all the students' suggestions, the speaker shares what he ultimately did. By this time, the students are vested in the outcome.

Other times, my co-mentor and I taught by using the case method with a project he had invested in called "Hydration Pack," a product that could purify polluted water. Students became immediately fascinated with the product and liked brainstorming the different applications and needs for purified water. He brought a sample of the product into class and passed it around for the students to touch and feel.

The following is the business dilemma that Phil presented to the class:

The company's manufacturing plant had burned down and the head of the company was at a crossroad in terms of how to move forward—should he rebuild the plant or outsource production? With many disasters, such as floods, tsunamis, and hurricanes, there could be a greater need for faster distribution and quantity manufacturing.

The students became integrated into this problem. What should the CEO do and what decisions were in the balance? The following is the exercise given to the students (listed by timing and content). They were divided by departments of a typical business, given difficult questions to ponder, and asked to give their recommendations to the CEO before hearing what the company actually did.

Case Method Exercise: Hydration Pack

Following is a timeline for a case study class. Obviously, this is simplified from the classic Harvard methodology, but this was the version we found worked with our class. The elements of this case study should be readily adaptable to any profession.

To prepare for this class, write a one-to-two page professional synopsis that describes the product and the dilemma you are focusing on. In this case it should include the history of the product, its current use, sales to date, and a description of how the plant was destroyed by a fire (or any problem therein). Before students arrive, write on the board a chart of the company's departmental questions (see chart below).

9:00 a.m. Students take turns reading aloud the two-page synopsis of the product and the dilemma.

9:10 a.m. The presenter refers to the chart drawn in advance on the board, which details the company's different departments and their various responsibilities. He explains to the students that they will be divided into these five departments and should listen closely. For the next twenty minutes the leader explains each department and the questions listed, giving examples or quandaries to illuminate ideas. These departments and issues should be universally relevant.

Chart of Departmental Questions

Sales Department

Option 1: Should outside representatives or distributors be used, or should the product be sold directly to consumers using an internal sales team?

Option 2: Should the product be priced per unit or per a certain quantity?

Option 3: Depending on what you decide above, please determine what price your product would be sold for wholesale and retail.

Marketing Department

Option 1: Determine who is the best target audience for this product—the government, corporations, retail outlets, or consumers who would buy it directly? Explain why.

Option 2: Explain how you would position the product—what need would it fill and what makes it unique.

Option 3: Evaluate whether you would use public relations or advertising to market the product.

Legal Department

Option: Determine whether you would apply for a worldwide patent on the product or protect it as a trade secret.

Finance Department

Options for investment:
   a. $3 million investment for 30 percent ownership
   b. $5 million investment for 51 percent ownership
   c. No investment, slow growth based on sales

Operations Department

Option 1: Should the product be manufactured in-house or externally?
Option 2: Should it be produced in the United States or abroad?

9:30 a.m. The presenter tells the students the CEO of Hydration Pack is in a quandary. He needs advice from all his departments on how to move forward and grow the company.

The class then divides into five groups according to the departments listed on the board and are instructed to discuss their recommended choice for fifteen to twenty minutes. It is critical that they also understand what the other departments are recommending because they are interdependent. If manufacturing is going to be in-house in the United States, this will affect what it costs to make the product, which will affect its price. The location of manufacturing will also affect the ability to have a quick turnaround, which will impact the audience you want to serve. For example, if Hydration Pack's audience was the Federal Emergency Management Agency, the company would need the capacity to fill a large order quickly in the event of an emergency.

9:50 a.m. The students pick a spokesperson from each group and present their findings, providing three primary reasons to back up their choice.

10:15 a.m. The presenter leads the discussion on how the students' choices would work together or what could go wrong if they followed the proposed class recommendations.

Now is an excellent time to share the action the company actually took. The case method gives students the ability to wrap their arms around a complex problem, work collaboratively, understand the big picture of how decisions are made, engage in professional dialogue, apply judgment, arrive at a well-considered solution, and communicate that solution to others. This is a great template to work from for your product, service, or industry.

Marketing-Your-Product

This program was developed by several members of NFTE D.C.'s board of directors, all of us marketing professionals: Cheryl Dickinson, vice president of R2i; Minal Damani Kundra, formerly at AOL and Discovery Education; and me. This exercise offers students an introduction to the concept of marketing and the part it plays in our everyday lives.

9:00 a.m. Introduce yourself and your relevant experience.

9:35 a.m. Explain some background concepts and present a few examples.

- Present the concepts of:
  - *Brand awareness:* How does a brand develop? What methods are used to build product recognition and familiarity?

- *Point of Purchase:* What drivers bring a purchaser to close a deal? How do you get a consumer to buy a product?
- *Retention:* What do companies do to keep you coming back and buying more? How do they keep you as a client?
- Cite examples of commercial products that are targeted to the age group in the class—for example, Apple, Coca-Cola, and McDonald's.
- Discuss how companies employ marketing strategies and tactics to reach an audience.

9:40 a.m. Explore how marketing is all around us, even in schools. Ask the students:

- What activities are you aware of at school, and how did you hear about them?
  (For example, sports games, clothing sales, after-school clubs)
- What activities are considered cool, and why?
  (For example, yearbook committee, cheerleading, football, weight training)
- Why did you select the classes you are currently taking?
- Who influenced you?

9:50 a.m. Ask the students to choose a product, program, or service and describe it, including its history, how it was developed, and the audience it serves. (We selected the NFTE program as an in-school marketing project to build awareness among students.)

9:55 a.m. Have a group discussion exercise on increasing demand for a product.

- Divide the students into three groups—awareness, purchase, and retention—and have them appoint a note taker and presenter. The goals will be:
  1. Building awareness: How do we build familiarity and name recognition with an audience?

2. Purchasing a product: How do we get an audience engaged in actually buying a product? Discuss the transaction.

3. Retention: How do we keep that buyer coming back for more purchases?

- The presenter should circulate and help students develop tactics.

10:10 a.m. Each group spends five minutes presenting their ideas and recommendations.

10:25 a.m. Summarize and discuss real-life outcomes from a company, citing examples of awareness, purchase, and retention. You can weave in any articles of interest on the topic.

The Art of the Interview: How to Tell a Story and Build Your Brand

I had the opportunity to speak with one of the Washington, D.C., area's most prolific educators, Dr. Jeff Kudisch. He walks the line daily between the business sector and academia, and has mapped out a robust program that pairs executive coaches with his students to better prepare students for their careers. An industrial psychologist by training, Kudisch is the assistant dean and managing director of the Office of Career Services at the Robert H. Smith School of Business at the University of Maryland. Kudisch is also a faculty expert on business leadership, and he writes a monthly column for the *Washington Post*.

Kudisch provided me with the excellent pointers he uses to prepare students for job interviews. His secret is to have them tell a story as a means of sharing their passions. As a matter of fact, he likes to guide students to find their passion through several assessment tools. One he mentioned, which I will share with you, is Gallup's Clifton StrengthsFinder assessment. For $15, a student can take an exam and self-identify her top five dominant talents. In addition, Kudisch asks students to find their "flow," which he defines as "when an individual is engrossed and lost in what they are doing, where time vanishes." I have been inspired by Kudisch's words, how he helps students find their path, and have woven in some of my own consulting experiences to create the following class exercise, designed for students to better present themselves.

Creating Your Personal Brand Exercise

How do we prepare ourselves to go for an interview? How do we put our best foot forward and make a good first impression? The following exercise will better prepare your mentees to think about themselves and their own unique brand needs.

9:00 a.m. Explain the context of the exercise to the students: in an interview situation, an interviewer often looks to a person's past performance as a predictor of her future performance. In this type of "behavioral job interview," an employer tries to assess whether candidates have experienced situations, organizations, cultures, and projects similar to ones they would encounter at the company.

Citi senior vice president Joseph Colca said that effective interviewees are prepared with a library of personal branding. Interviewers want to know if a candidate communicates in a way that is clear and concise, and can convey how her background fits the position and how she would add value to the company.

9:05 a.m. Distribute a handout or write the following highlights on the board and discuss:

- Be prepared, but don't over-rehearse. Have an arsenal of stories ready, depending on how the interview goes.
- Be mindful. Listen to the interviewer's questions carefully and remain positive.
- Be memorable, and show enthusiasm. People remember unique anecdotes, especially ones that convey emotion and show how you have overcome fear. One effective technique is to name the story; say, "I'd like to share the 'ice cream story.'"

- Be prepared for tricky questions, such as: What is the riskiest decision you have made? What kinds of people do you have trouble working with? Why should I hire you?
- Be positive, even if the question seems to seek the negative—for example, you might be asked a question about how you deal with obstacles. You can incorporate a modified outcome and learned takeaways. Such questions or prompts could include, "Tell me a time when you failed. Tell me a time when you missed a solution to a problem."
- Be the star, use "I," and emphasize a key role you played in delivering results. Don't focus on circumstances or use terms where you "helped." Be action oriented.
- Be the icing on the cake; organizations are looking for employees to be curious, to have a thirst for learning, and to display a passion for growth.

Consider Kudisch's final statement, "*Remember, stellar resumes land interviews, stellar stories land jobs.*"

Confidence and Body Language

Part and parcel in preparing students for their first interview—for designing their unique brand—is to also discuss their style, poise, demeanor. How are we perceived is a conglomeration of our packaging, not just our words.

9:20 a.m. As the presenter, share your personal experiences and discuss appropriate behavior and conduct, body language, and making a positive, lasting first impression. Explore the concept that actions and appearance often speak louder than words.

Introduction and Handshake

- Invite a student to the front of the class and, as the leader, introduce yourself and model first *what not to do*, and then *what to do*:
    1. Say your first and last name under your breath, give a limp handshake, don't make eye contact, stand hunched over, and look

uncertain. *Ask the selected student her impression of your behavior and what it says about you.*

2. Then, introduce yourself again using a strong, confident voice, stand up straight, look the student in the eye, and shake her hand firmly. Ask again what her impression is.

- Ask the entire class to stand up, pick a partner, and introduce themselves with a firm handshake, standing tall and making direct eye contact. Walk around the room and observe the students' introductions.

Dressing and Looking the Part

- Attire: Discuss options for appropriate attire for a job interview. Begin a conversational dialogue about what to wear to an interview for a job in an office environment (or a retail store) by holding up magazine photos of different styles. Ask the class, "What does your attire say to your potential employer? What is the message you are conveying if you wear examples x-y-z?"
- Discuss the importance of:

Cleanliness: Neat and washed hair, clean nails, clean and pressed clothes.

Moderation: Err on the side of moderation in dress and appearance. Wear neutral or dark-colored clothing such as white, navy, gray, or beige, and modest jewelry.

Proper dress: For example, men should wear long pants, a belt, a button-down shirt, a blazer, and usually a tie. Women should wear dress slacks or a knee-length skirt with a blouse and possibly a blazer, or a dress. They should also wear low heels, not stilettos.

Being on time: Showing up on time is one of the most important ways to make a good impression. It shows that you care and are reliable, and that the interview and job are important to you. Ask the class: if you are supposed to meet someone and he is twenty to thirty minutes late, what is the message he is conveying to you? How does it feel to be kept waiting?

The thank-you note: I always recommend that the student send some form of thank-you note within one or two days of the interview. In it, recap the highlights and how important the position is to you, how much you enjoyed meeting your interviewer, and how you look forward to hearing back about the interesting opportunity.

9:35 a.m. Present rules for storytelling. If students have not had a job, their stories will be drawn from internships, projects, hobbies, or extracurricular activities. The most important thing is that students share takeaways of *what they learned* rather than all the details.

Kudisch suggests keeping a story to three minutes: thirty seconds to state the problem or issue, a minute and a half to describe the interviewee's role in solving the problem and what he did, and one minute to discuss results, consequences, and/or takeaways.

Story Example: Leadership

I'd like to share with you my "ice cream" story.

Problem: I was working behind the counter for my summer job when I was sixteen. My main role was scooping ice cream and giving samples. I'd only been there three weeks when the manager of my store had an emergency and had to leave. There were only two of us on that day plus the cleaning person. It was ninety degrees out, and the store was packed. I assured my manager that I could handle it.

Implementation: Well, I scooped double time. I made a tray of samples for the cleaning person to pass to customers while they waited in line. I explained to the customers that we had a small emergency, and wait time would be just a little bit longer, but the afternoon flew by with no crisis.

Result: When my manager returned and saw the number of sales on the cash register, she immediately promoted me to assistant manager.

My takeaway: I learned that I can handle pressure situations, and that if I'm honest, customers will understand.

9:45–10:00 a.m. Choose one of the following exercises:

In-Class Writing Exercise on Self-Branding through Storytelling

- Using the rules for storytelling outlined above, have the students spend five minutes writing about one experience where they think they excelled and showed leadership, teamwork, or creativity.
- Have students break into groups of two for five minutes and share their stories with each other.
- As a class, discuss their experience, what they learned from this, what made them uncomfortable, and any questions they have about shaping their stories and presenting them.
- A future assignment might be to develop and perfect one story and come back to share it aloud with the class.
- Another assignment could be to produce a portfolio of stories that highlight different characteristics, creating eight different short stories. In our conversation, Kudisch suggested that students be prepared on these topics: leadership, integrity, creativity, communication, teamwork, critical thinking, motivation, and adaptability.

Group Exercise in Class and Individual Homework Assignment on Preparing for Interviews

- Ask the class to divide into partners.
- Hand out interview questions from real executives (see below).
- Each participant in the duo should take a turn being the executive interviewer.
- Each interviewee should, to the best of his ability, answer the questions posed.
- For homework, ask the students to write their own positive and concise stories based on an experience; then discuss each student's answer in class. This exercise helps students discover they have all had actual experiences that have prepared them for the working world, and which they can share with potential employers.

- There is a column called "Openers" in the *New York Times* Sunday business section in which a CEO of a company answers the question, "How do you hire?" The following are hard-to-answer interview questions that should be passed out, one per twosome. These are from chief executive officers of Accenture, Kaiser Permanente, Yahoo, and Smartsheet.com.
  - What adversity have you had to face and how did you handle it?
  - How have you shown an ability to synthesize information and act?
  - How do you relate to people?
  - How do you get people excited about doing something?
  - If you are hired, in six months, we will know each other much better. What will your team and I say you do very well? What will we say we wish you did better? Do not say, "You will love everything about me."
  - What motivates you?
  - What would your enemies say about you? And if you don't think you have any enemies, pretend you do.

Other Ideas for Leading the Class

Leading a class is an exercise in creativity. The following are a few more ideas to stimulate your thinking for bringing your unique experiences to class. (Please feel free to share new ideas with us as well, on our web site, www.teachtowork.com, or blog.)

Do a Blind Taste Test

We conducted this exercise when we were studying Honest Tea and its growth as a new product. I brought in several flavors of iced tea products—Paul Newman's, Snapple, Tazo, and others—and covered the bottles. The students sampled each product blindfolded and chose their favorite without being influenced by the brand. Honest Tea is not as sweet as its competitors, and was not the favored product in our taste test. We discussed the company's growth, its buyout by Coca-Cola, and how the company marketed to an educated consumer who was more interested in health than in a supersweet product. This generated a lot of conversation among the students.

Design an Interview for Consumers

Design a five-point questionnaire that students will have to lead either with other members of their class or with the outside world. Example: create twenty favorite components for designing your own fast food restaurant. Design a questionnaire with a list of characteristics and interview ten people. By doing so, students will learn which elements are most in demand and improve the likelihood of sales for their new restaurant. Students should assemble the responses and present their hypotheses as well as their conclusions.

Conduct a Show-and-Tell Marketing Exercise

I often prepare a marketing exercise by showing, in depth, creativity in packaging and marketing. It's been great fun over the years, and students seem to remember the activity in their year end letters. I ask all the students to form a close circle around me, because I have many things to pass around and share. Each presentation (7 minutes each) represents a different form of marketing (i.e., co-branding, packaging, upselling, creating demand). The following are a few examples.

Georgetown Cupcakes is a D.C.-based company that burgeoned quickly and that students know. I presented their brand by showing the variety of ways they present themselves. I brought to class swirled stickers, pink boxes for cupcakes, weekly calendar of flavors, gift card packages, photos of their stores, clips from their TV show, articles about their first vision and growth model, and taste samples. The students were immersed in a full campaign based on one product line.

The artists Christo and his wife and partner Jeanne-Claude provide another fascinating story. The way they raised money by making renderings of their installations was remarkable. I bring in books to pass around and we talk about Christo and Jeanne-Claude's unique process for creating demand, noting that his preinstallation drawings became significantly more expensive after the three-week installations were taken down.

Indeed, I have held on to a fabulous article about the Washington Redskins owner, Dan Snyder. The article takes us through, step by step, how he paid for a franchise, built a stadium, and proceeded to create value, stratify seating categories, create revenue streams in off season times, and sell naming rights. The students love football, but never had an in-depth understanding of how it is a business. We simply take turns reading from the article, and discuss as we go.

Guest Speakers

There are many factors to consider when choosing a guest speaker or speakers, such as:

- Whom to choose, based on topic, project, or timing with the curriculum
- Whether to invite one speaker or a panel of speakers
- When in the semester/year to invite a speaker
- How to best prepare speakers; ideally, you should help plan their visits and discuss what they should do and/or bring
- Other roles guests can play during the year

Many successful individuals have been in the role of protégé themselves and relish the opportunity to pay something back. You want to find speakers who have a genuine interest in the program's goals and a desire to participate. Best of all would be someone who has an interest in playing an ongoing role in your mentoring efforts.

You should also be looking for people who:

- Have a *good story* to tell, such as overcoming adversity, struggling in a new environment or country, or dealing with physical or emotional challenges

- Demonstrate success in a field that will interest the kids or is a field they can *relate to*
- Have the ability to *connect* with students. Having been a parent may help qualify a person to deal with youth, but being empathetic, patient, and a good communicator are all key—as is, of course, being the kind of person whose behavior sets them up as a *role model.*

Age is irrelevant. Successful and motivating individuals can be great speakers whether they are just embarking on their career, are well established, or are on the cusp of retirement.

Coordinate with the teacher, who should prepare students in advance of the guest speaker's arrival and provide them with a speaker bio. When appropriate, the teacher can ask students to prepare questions in advance and even assign a grade to students based on their participation, their behavior, and perhaps even a summary report of what they learned from the guest speaker.

When to Fit Speakers into the Schedule

Bringing in speakers is an inspiring way to kick off the school year. It motivates the students and helps them get past their fear of coming up with ideas for their projects, and generally builds enthusiasm for the curriculum ahead. If the guest speaker's story can relate to the students' specific assignment, so much the better.

If the speaker appears at the beginning of the term, you can refer to her advice throughout the year for ideas about how to operate.

Preparing Guest Speakers

It is very useful to meet with speakers ahead of their class visit to go over logistics and a plan for the day. Or, you could arrange to meet before the class in an empty classroom or other space. Make sure you have everyone's contact information, and that all speakers have yours, should you need to get in touch the day of their visit.

If anyone asks what to wear, suggest that he dress to represent what he does for a living. Some will come in suits, some in business casual, and others in jeans and eccentric accessories.

Planning Your Guest's Visit

The following are factors to discuss with your guest in advance.

What to Bring

Props, visuals, marketing materials, anything tangible goes a long way with students. Encourage your guest speakers to be creative, and to think about how they can "show" what they do and not just talk about it.

How to Present

Depending on the speaker's comfort level, she can speak to the class on her own or, as the class mentor, you can act as an interviewer.

Most successful individuals did not come straight from "Planet Success"; they had to work to get where they are. Tell your speaker to use this opportunity to shed her façade and bare her soul to the students. Some tips to share with your guest:

- Share your own high school experience. Or, talk about the first dollar you earned. Both of these examples will help the kids relate to you and narrow the gap between you.
- Tom Brown, a former teacher at Anacostia High School in Washington, D.C., advises, "Don't bring your 'success story.' Tell the students the worst experience you've had and how you resolved it. Also tell them your best one and what it meant to you."
- You can connect with the students by sharing your emotions, struggles, or obstacles. You can also share why you love what you do.
- What was the seminal moment that brought you to the idea of the business you are in? What were your fears? What were your qualifications? What made you feel you could do this? Did you have a mentor?

- What do you love about your business or profession? Relate what you do to the students' experience, if possible.
- Tell specific stories about a client, such as the best client you ever had and how you won their business.
- Talk about a marketing package or big project. Did you have competitors? How did you determine an audience for a product? How did you decide on a niche?
- It is good for kids to have an association with money. Share the costs associated with starting your business or the salary range associated with your profession.

More Tips for Presenting

Test these tips when speaking to your mentees, and pass on the most pertinent to your guest speaker. Prepare your speakers for success, both for their sake and so the students will get the greatest benefit from their presentation. Suggest that speakers:

- Arrive early and try to connect with a few students, learn some names, and inquire about the kids' interests and hobbies.
- Speak in language at the level of the kids' understanding, not in industry jargon or technical language. Avoid being preachy. Kids relate better to authentic stories, decisions, and feelings.
- Stay aware of whether kids are becoming fidgety; if they are, ask some questions to keep them on their toes, change your pace or tone, and have fun! Students these days often have short attention spans, and it may take some effort to keep them engaged.

One Speaker or Several at a Time?

Depending on your field and the length of the class, you may want to bring in a single speaker or a panel. For a ninety-minute class, you could have three speakers presenting for twenty minutes each and leave thirty minutes for questions. Or you could have a single speaker who might present some kind of visual aid, learning activity, or game for that length of time and go more in-depth with the kids.

For one class, I invited a distributor of national hair products to speak. Not only did he bring samples of his products, but since the students were quite familiar with the products, they had a lively conversation about the pros and cons.

As part of his presentation, the distributor explained the roles of the manufacturers, distributors, and retailers in getting products made and to market. My co-mentor and I decided to take advantage of what he taught by having the kids play a game under his guidance. After his presentation, we divided the kids into three groups and asked them to come up with questions for the other groups.

The retailers asked the distributors things like: Why should I buy this? Will you offer training? How will you assist in advertising, packaging, and displays?

The distributors asked the manufacturers: What kind of volume do you manufacture on a monthly basis? Can you provide adequate training that speaks to your advantages over your competition? What kind of fleets do you have for delivery?

The manufacturers asked the retailers questions such as: How can we improve our product? Can you tell us more about the nature of your buyer? Do you recommend any sales promotions? What is the price point per item or per quantity?

Playing that game helped the students learn about how goods come to market in a dynamic fashion. This game concept could be a teaching tool to raise students' awareness of many other processes as they relate to any number of goods and services. Consider these ideas:

- An architect could divide the groups into homeowners, architects/designers, and contractors. An interesting presentation would be to learn how their fields vary, how they work together, and what are their differing priorities. You could even break up kids into three categories, and have them role play from the perspective of their group.

- A panel including a drug manufacturer/researcher, a distributor, and a pharmacist (or any one of them) could explain how product development is done in the pharmaceutical field. Just like the homeowner panel, students could learn about how a product is developed, and how interdependent the sectors are on each other, and how a product comes to market. I always suggest that students integrate with the material if they take on the role as an exercise.
- Another panel might consist within technology, including a hardware manufacturer, software designer, and business end user. Students today are so involved with the Internet—visiting speakers that align within an industry demonstrate the chain of development and interdependence.

A Panel of Guest Speakers

Another speaking panel can be diverse. I have assembled a panel of guest speakers from completely different backgrounds and brought out the similarities in their priorities. Panels have included, for example, the owner of a pizza franchise, a ceramicist, a software developer, and a cofounder of an electric bicycle start-up company.

Pizza Franchise Owner

The students had never heard of the franchise concept, so they were intrigued to learn from the pizza store owner that it was possible to buy another company's idea and recipes. They were also interested in his story: he had failed at a previous real estate development career impacted by the recession. He had to reinvent himself as a pizza store owner, but he was happy to have found a product that he believes in and was willing to pay for the use of. It was a revelation to the students that you don't necessarily have to come up with the best and most unique idea, but can be equally successful with a franchise industry! They were wowed to learn the speaker had franchised ten locations, and he totally won them over when he brought in pizzas to sample.

Ceramicist

This artist/business owner taught the kids about the process of producing an item from scratch and bringing it to market. She brought in unformed clay, an unfinished clay plate, a painted clay plate, and a fired clay plate, making every step of the process tangible. She discussed her role in making the products, producing them on a wider scale, and then distributing them to fifty retailers across the country. She gave the students some insight into the dilemmas even successful businesspeople face when she explained she was trying to decide whether to produce all her items in-house or have them manufactured on a wider scale in China.

Software Developer

The software designer's story was compelling because it started when he was a sixteen-year-old living in India. He wrote a blog on how he thought software should work. Someone from Silicon Valley saw the blog, e-mailed him, and offered him a job. Now, he employs two thousand employees. The students were delighted to hear a story of transformation from a person who had actually experienced it, having been plucked from a village in India and set down in Silicon Valley.

Bicycle Company Owner

All eyes were on Amber Wason as she wheeled a sleek, prototype electric bicycle into the classroom. "Riide" is her new company that manufactures electric bikes. It is a cutting-edge example for filling a niche—for an easy source of transportation for urban people who want to ride their bikes to work, arrive with no sweat, and not necessarily don spandex from head to toe to manage hills. Wason drove home to the students that "it is okay to fail" and that Riide is not her first effort. She explained that to get to where she is today—on the verge of delivering Riide bikes to the first 120 customers who preordered them—took years of testing, research, and fundraising. Wason decided to be an entrepreneur after losing her job, and her cofounder has sunk most of his savings into the company.

"We have had a lot of luck, and done a lot of hard work," Wason told the students. She added, "We had a lot of awesome mentors," and stressed, "Believing in your product is very important." In order to start your own business, "You find a way to sacrifice," Wason said.

Roles for Returning Guest Speakers

Often a guest speaker will want to return for more mentor-style visits. The following is a list of other roles they can perform, prior to taking on the full mentor role.

- Field trip sponsor or chaperone
- Provider of project oversight
- Presentation coach
- Competition judge

Field Trips

Field trips are a crucial element in exposing students "physically" to another world. There are a number of factors to consider when choosing a destination and planning the field trip, including:

- Time off from school: coordinate a date with the class teacher
- Permission slips: teachers can help draft and have permission slips sent home for parent signatures
- Transportation: discuss viable options with the teacher, such as a bus paid for by the school, transportation funded by the mentor, or public transportation

In addition to these practical considerations of orchestrating the trip, there are a multitude of options for field trips or buying trips. In the following sections, we'll look at some of the types of trips students might find engaging or useful in advancing their projects.

One Site: Operation Tour, Lunch, or Trade Show

Each year, a representative from E-Trade, a financial services company, offered to host a field trip for my class at its Northern Virginia facility. After each trip, E-Trade received letters from my students saying they "never thought banking could be so cool," and they "never imagined themselves working in banking until they went on that field trip."

Over the course of four hours, the students toured the different departments with a company spokesman. They learned about each department, heard about what the company did, and got a feel for the physical space.

During one of the trips, the students displayed their business projects, and company employees interacted with the students and provided feedback and suggestions. This opportunity could be expanded so that the students publicly pitch their ideas to company employees. Company employees could be assigned one-to-one to the students and provide real-life feedback about student projects or even share their own professional trajectories.

During the trip, E-Trade generously hosted a pizza and salad lunch for the kids. Other companies have offered a brown bag or box lunch, and invited company speakers to come in and talk to the students.

Multiple Sites

Another option for a field trip is to tour multiple sites. Choose sites that would be educational and/or project related. Be creative, and think about what you have access to, who you know, and what would be inspiring for the students. Some examples include:

Architecture
Visit three homes or businesses that you (or your company) have designed. When showing the physical space, discuss a challenge that existed, how you solved the problem, how long the project took to design and construct, and what the result was.

Real Estate Developer

Share photos of what a site looked like when it was acquired, and go through some of the rents per square foot that tenants paid. Then take a field trip to look at the site today. New signage, lighting, and sidewalks show how the developer improved the site and the neighborhood, and how rents have changed.

Big Brothers Big Sisters

In the School without Walls Program in the Philadelphia school system, students are bused twice a week to major employers in the area. Students visit with one designated mentor over lunch. They are exposed to new environments and to conversations with new adults on a recurring basis.

Buying Trip

Mentors in the NFTE program take their students on a wholesale buying trip. The students get seed capital and head to a wholesale district in New York City to buy goods related to their project.

Students are taught negotiation skills. They begin to understand the concept of "buy low and sell high" and to realize that the lower the price point of the supplies or components you buy, the higher your own profit margin.

Other examples of a buying trip could involve taking students to buy drafting pencils or other materials necessary to execute their project and to interact with vendors in that profession.

Trade Shows and Sales

In my early days with NFTE, we arranged several opportunities for students to integrate with environments that were foreign to them. One such outlet was a **holiday showcase** that took place in a downtown office building. Students set up sales booths and practiced their business pitches with real buyers. A mix of NFTE board members, donors, and supporters, as well as employees from the office buildings, passed through and bought products or inquired about the students' business plans.

Science fairs are an excellent way to bring students to new worlds and give them a chance to talk with others about their ideas and projects. The Intel International Science and Engineering Fair, for example, which is held in a different city each year, provides a terrific opportunity for students to learn and be inspired.

Following are some other options for students to integrate with their communities:

- **Fashion shows** hosted by large department stores bring an audience and provide a space for design students to attend who are learning the art of fashion.
- **Conventions** that focus on specific subjects provide additional opportunities. You could schedule a field trip to a food show, health expo, technology fair, or interior design or industrial design convention. Many industry trades would be delighted to open their doors for a class looking to learn about their product or service.
- **Restaurants** are often willing to take students on a tour of their kitchens during off hours to show how they prepare for a night. Students learn about storage, refrigeration, preparation, and presentation.
- **Television, radio, and newspaper** public relations directors will often open the doors to their headquarters and lead behind-the-scene tours to give students an insider's view of how the news and other features are produced.

Knowing the project target, having minimal funds for transportation and admission, and exposing students to new places and potential careers is absolutely eye opening for them. The community, if asked, will often welcome your student visitors. It is up to each of us to make it happen.

Recap

In this chapter, we explored many ways for mentors to expose students to experiences outside the realm of their everyday lives. We discussed:

- Collaborating side by side
- Leading a class with your expertise
- Designing student games that teach critical thinking
- Developing a branding narrative for interviews
- Sharing life stories and trajectories of guest speakers
- Taking field trips or touring project-related industries for research

All these efforts bring the professional world to the classroom and make it tangible through you, the mentor. Whether you visit weekly, bimonthly, monthly, or six times a year, the experiences you share can alter a student's perspective and be both emotionally and physically transformative.

Note

1. Steve Mariotti, "How Giving Back Can Heal," *Huffington Post*, August 16, 2013, accessed March 27, 2016, http://www.huffingtonpost.com/steve-mariotti/how-giving-back-can-heal-_b_3764058.html.

CHAPTER 10

THE ART OF PRESENTING

Turning Students into Teachers

We are all teachers. Teaching is the core of humanity. It is what life is all about, passing it on—sometimes intentionally, sometimes skillfully, sometimes neither. We teach to articulate for ourselves what matters. We teach to be sure that we have not lived in vain. We teach to learn.[1]

—Eric Liu, author of *Guiding Lights:
How to Mentor and Find Life's Purpose*

One of the most exciting phases of Project Based Mentoring is preparing the student to present her body of work publicly. The student becomes the knowledgeable one, defending her project's course of study and conclusions. At this juncture, you will note a marked shift, as the relationship is no longer just you, your student, and the project. Now there is a fourth dimension: an audience. Inevitably, the student experiences a keen vulnerability, knowing she has to present in front of people and be judged.

This chapter is about how to prepare your mentee for presenting her project before a group of peers and adults in a competitive arena. For each year I have mentored, I have been told that the task of presenting is the students' crowning achievement in their minds. Comments recur annually such as, "I never thought I could do this," "I have gained so much confidence now that I've learned I can talk in front of others," "I'm so proud to have overcome my fear and present like I did," and "I learned so much from watching my classmates present." Over and over again, in letters or at the year-end recap, students and their grateful parents all proclaim this new skill a barrier broken.

Think about it. How many times are fourteen- to nineteen-year-olds asked to select a project, research it, understand findings, design and implement a plan, demonstrate use, know the potential impact on an audience, review opposing or competitive points of view, and defend the project publicly? This assignment is quite different from researching a paper topic and writing in a theoretical vacuum. The project based presentation comingles with experience in the professional world.

Indeed, this end-of-year assignment has many transformational qualities: it builds communication skills students can use for the rest of their lives. It pushes students to deliver fact-based knowledge in a professional, concise manner. How valuable is that skill throughout life? Here are a few examples:

- When asking for a raise and defending your accomplishments
- When requesting increased funding before a board
- When reporting on an assignment to a body of peers
- When trying to persuade clients of a new approach you recommend

In these examples, the ability to assemble one's thoughts, be concise, and be verbally persuasive is a big asset in the professional world.

"Slap Some Cheese on It!"

For the most part, students do not instinctively know how to make a presentation. Consider Bruce and Glen, twins who were part of the first NFTE class Phil and I ever mentored, in 2001. We still stay in touch. Their backstory reflects pain and difficulty. The brothers were from a challenged family with little means. Dad was incarcerated for drug dealing and had left their mom to raise three kids alone. Their upbringing was augmented by a stern, ever-present grandmother and reinforced by an active neighborhood church community. The twins were spirited despite their adversities. They were high energy, artistically talented, fashion forward, musical, handsome, funny, and popular—the whole shebang *times two*.

They called their business "Twin Sports." They took $1 black T-shirts, cut and folded them into ten cloth headbands that they hand designed with glitter and urban slang. To me, they looked a bit like graffiti on your head with words such as: "Street Beats," "Urban-hood" or "Victory for Vikings" (the school team). The cost to make each headband was forty-one cents. Bruce and Glen walked around the school not only wearing their own product, they also designed a portable display, a creative two-foot by three-foot decorative piece of cardboard that was filled with product. (Think eyeglass display case, baiting customers to try on a pair and check themselves out in an attached mini mirror.) Thanks to their charismatic personalities and their craft, within three months fifteen hundred of the school's population (about half) were wearing these new-fangled fashions, glittered headbands that sold for $4 each. You do the math.

Bruce and Glen learned the concept of entrepreneurship quickly. They experienced success and earned play money to boot. But when they were asked to present their business plan to the rest of the class and to four judges, we were shocked: for all that energy, personality, and success, their presentation fell flat. Why? We didn't understand.

The twins made it to the finals anyway because of their phenomenal sales history and the business plan they had executed. They knew how to be *in* business, but not how to *discuss* it in a professional manner. As their mentors, we knew they weren't yet vested in the presentation. They were timid, reticent, holding back. Maybe it was the classroom? The packaging? The jargon? Or was just being judged that was putting them off? We couldn't let them retreat. The game wasn't over; it was just starting.

After several more rounds of coaching, rehearsal sessions, and motivational conversations, the boys shared with us that now they were "in it to win it." Our task, essentially, was to remove their fear. We knew they could tell their own story uniquely if their creativity and natural savvy could be unleashed. Ultimately, they underwent an attitude shift. To quote the twins, they decided to, "Slap some cheese on it!"

The difference between their first presentation in the classroom and the one they gave for the semifinals and then the finals was like night and day.

While the competition was stiff—they were going head to head against five of the best young entrepreneurs in the whole mid-Atlantic region—Bruce and Glen got up in front of the group and did their "twin thing" as only they could!

"I'm Bruce . . . (pause)," "and I'm Glen . . . (pause)." Then they'd slap, slap, slap—performing a fast-paced, patty-cake hand thing—and follow with a sharp, choreographed turn to the audience, a flash of huge, beautiful smiles, and, fingers pointed straight at the judges, chimed together in a punctuated chorus: "And we are Twin Sports!" After that opening, they had everyone in the palm of their hands! It was time to get down to business. They knew their material cold, streamlined their talk to relevant sound bites, and stole the show.

Bruce and Glen took home a $1,500 check for first place. Our hearts were in our throats! And we became hooked on this new calling: mentorship.

Selling Your Ideas

I believe the most important learning that takes place in the Project Based Mentoring process is the final presentation. Why?

- It makes the student the teacher.
- It forces the student to hone presentation materials and to be succinct.
- It creates a deeper understanding and ownership of the content.
- It pushes the student to view ideas from an audience's point of view.
- It allows the student to integrate ideas with others and receive questions and feedback.
- It fosters confidence and respect in a public arena.

Simulating a Work Relationship

By the time you start working with a student on his final presentation (hopefully two months before the presentation date), you already know him. You understand the project and its goals. You have a unique vantage point: you have earned the student's trust, and, most importantly, you are an experienced practitioner in the project field. You are a vested collaborator. Indeed, you or your company might have even funded the expenses for the class project.

It's important to understand that, up to this point, adult relationships in a student's life may have been limited. They might include parents, relatives, teachers, neighbors, clergy, or guidance counselors. Of course, all are well-intentioned authority figures. But, when *you* say to your mentee, "You can do it," "This looks really good," "This is shaping up nicely," or "This is competitive," your words carry a different weight. They convey a message honed by experience and interaction. Your words are independent and respected. You do not fit into any of the prior adult relationship categories.

My best public example of a working mentor relationship that crosses generations would actually be from the TV program, *The Voice*. A sixteen-year-old mentee may have heard from a church music director, or a high school choral instructor, or a parent that she has talent. Of course she is encouraged. But the message is resoundingly different when Adam Levine, Gwen Stefani, Pharrell Williams, or Blake Shelton says, "Kid, you really have talent." Think about it. A similar effect applies to the student who is working in a field of your expertise.

I know this because I have interviewed students extensively on their relationship to their project mentor. You differ because you are in a working relationship. You are not automatically biased toward them like a relative. Nor are you grading them, admonishing them, or punishing them like a teacher. You are not lecturing them on integrity, ethics, or religion from a pulpit like a clergyperson. You are a consultant, listening and giving them undivided one-on-one time. You have a purpose to your dynamic that is non-emotional; rather, your attention is project focused. Essentially, you represent, for the student, a completely new form of adult relationship—that of a collaborator. You are simulating a work experience where age does not matter but content, delivery, and effort do.

Pick and Choose Suggestions

The following list of ideas will help you coach students on their presentation skills. Please select the highlights that relate to the individual student you are mentoring. If you overburden her with too many things to do, you risk making her more insecure. (I relate to this with my golf teachers. Too much direction is overwhelming!) Your goal is to find a balance, mixing your praise—such as "You can do it," "You know your material," and "This is really good"—with specific hints on how to improve. Keep the following list with you and choose the most relevant, salient points for each individual student.

Review the Framework of the PowerPoint Presentation

As you mentor your student, keep in mind that the structure of the Power-Point is particularly valuable. It organizes the assignment and gives a framework for the presentation. The whole class fills out the same slides, yet there is room for creative interpretation.

Title of Project

1. *Problem*: Simply state the problem or need the project is addressing.
2. *Objective*: Describe the purpose of the project and how it will address the problem above.
3. *Audience:* Identify the primary and secondary audiences being reached, using demographic research. Students should be able to describe the project's anticipated impact on an audience.
4. *Implementation:* Present a timeline of activities, research, interactions, interviews, experiments, and the necessary budget for launching the project.
5. *Obstacles/objections/competition:* Describe problems that occurred during the project.

6. *Result/impact:* Develop a statement of conclusion: what the project has proven and how it has fulfilled the objective.

7. *Lessons learned/takeaway:* State what you learned throughout the project, noting what you could have done differently, what new skills you have acquired, and advice for others who would embark on a similar study.

These are the seven standard slides that apply to every student and project. There is also room for five creative slides, which may include a field trip collage, questionnaire design, press release, graphs, pie charts, project photos, and so forth. It is up to the teacher and mentor to adjust the overview project assignment and recommend outlines and bullet points that may help make the presentation more effective.

Prepare for the Oral Presentation

Following are some pointers that can help your mentee practice with a PowerPoint screen:

- NBC anchor Lester Holt, ABC anchor David Muir, and CBS anchor Scott Pelley all sit at a desk and report news. Behind them are active screens with photos, charts, poll results, and so forth. Do you ever see them turn around and look at the screen behind them?

- Students are often limited to an eight- to ten minute time frame for a PowerPoint presentation, and without coaching they don't know where or how to stand. Should they face the audience or turn sideways and face the screen? Left to their own devices, they might read the screen and forget there is an audience altogether. Solution: we suggest that each student get a stack of three-by-five-inch flashcards. Each card represents a screen and the chronology matches the PowerPoint page by page.

Here are a few tips for organizing the material and preparing for the presentation:

Tell a Story

PowerPoint is merely an organizing tool that helps tell a story. We tell students that they are not bound by the words on the screen at all. Audiences, including judges, can multitask, and can read what is on the screen behind the student while listening to the students' words, just as they do when they watch news anchors.

Make One Salient Point Per Screen

The overriding message for each screen should be narrowed down to a sentence or two. Then, if a student wants to point to a statistic or photo that is passed out in collateral material, or to make more information available on one of five creative slides, they have more time and the freedom to do so.

Practice, Practice, Practice

Once a student has his cards ready, he should practice *out loud*, in front of a mirror. We suggest students watch themselves, underline or highlight points they want to emphasize, and listen for inflections in their voices. They should become so familiar with their choice of words and the points they want to make that they begin to enjoy an ease and comfort because they have done it so often.

Design the Opening

Starting a presentation is often the hardest part. We have to contain our nerves, assess and connect with the audience, be enthusiastic, and remain focused on the task at hand: delivering a message. Bruce and Glen, the twins, decided to "slap some cheese on it," and play up their twin dynamic.

The rest of us can borrow techniques to capture attention from advertisers, actors, and comedians we see on television, online, or in live theater. As mentors, we might ask students to think about three to five times when someone has captured their attention, and about how the person did so. The following are some standard techniques employed by Madison Avenue advertisers, theatrical openers, or revered speakers that we like to share with students as they are working through in preparing their opening ideas:

- **Ask a question and play to audience fear.** For example, when trying to sell breath mints or mouthwash, ads ask: "Do you ever worry that you have bad breadth?" A photo shows a dating couple, implying a fear of rejection by the opposite sex.

- **Show empathy to an audience.** For instance, if the product presented is Lean Cuisine frozen meals and Ragu spaghetti sauce, the question might be, "How many of you get tired of the same dinners night after night yet have only twenty minutes to prepare a meal after work?" An image appears of a harried woman in her kitchen, just home from work.

- **Use an eye-catching icon.** Think of Geico with its gecko or Capital One with its Vikings. Attract attention with an unexpected animal or an out-of-context Viking.

- **Demonstrate effectiveness versus a competitor.** If the product being sold is OxiClean, for example, before-and-after photos show that if you use this product rather than a competitor's, your wash will come out much cleaner.

- **Be a storyteller.** Think of Hallmark cards, which deliver the right message at the right time. Hallmark captures relationships by communicating emotions. Touch an audience with a poignant or uplifting story.

- **Draw on history, heritage, or culture.** Consider the Greek yogurt Fage and how it is marketed as representing the old country and the culture of Greece, where eating fresh, homemade yogurt is part of growing up. Perhaps a student's project harkens back to old-world lifestyles and would benefit from that positioning.

Adopt a Positive Mindset

When we talk with the students about their final presentations, we always tell them:

- Be yourself.
- Trust your instincts.
- You know your material better than anyone else, and you have researched it, lived it. Now just tell your story.
- You are now the teacher. Your audience *wants* to learn what you've learned. Take them on your journey.
- The judges are on your side; they are listening to learn and to help, not to be critical.
- Have fun! It is much easier for judges to listen when the presenter is enjoying himself.
- As Nike says, "Just Do It."

Establish Expectations

It is important to prepare your students by setting the scene as much as possible so they will know what to expect.

- **Physical space.** Describe where the oral presentation will take place, whether it will be in a classroom, cafeteria, or office building.
- **Audience/judges.** The students will want to visualize the experience. It's good to describe the room layout, who will be in the audience, and typically how many judges are expected to be there.
- **Timing.** Students will need to know the time they have to present their projects. (For NFTE, for example, students are given 8.5 minutes each for their presentations.) Often, we have a timekeeper who lets students know when they have five minutes left and one minute left, so they can plan the balance of their presentations accordingly.
- **Questions.** The judges are allowed a finite amount of time for asking questions. (NFTE, for example, allows three minutes.) The questions following the oral presentation prove to be a great learning moment! The timekeeper also tracks the judges' questioning time, so the allotment is fair to all presenters.

- **Observing others.** Often, fellow students are silent observers. It is helpful for the growth of each student to watch her fellow classmates present and to share in their experience, growth, and oral commentary.

Body Language and Social Skills

My best advice to my fellow mentors is not to assume anything. After years of being adults in boardrooms, business meetings, and social engagements, we take for granted the social skills we have developed over time. It's helpful to touch on elements of presenting from the list below, either in front of the entire class or by extracting highlights that relate to the individual student on an as-needed basis. Suggested pointers might include:

1. Pre-Presentation

Get Rest
Try to get a full night's sleep before your presentation. It will equip you with energy and resilience.

Wear Appropriate Attire
Wear clean, pressed, neat clothes. Depending on your audience and your subject, you might dress more professionally or in character with your project. For instance, if you are a chef, don a chef's hat or apron. If you are designing costumes or fashion, wear an outfit of your design to demonstrate your ability. If you are doing science experiments, wear a lab coat. What is inappropriate? Clothing that is too sexy, too baggy, too dirty, too ripped, too short, or too bare.

Arrive Early
When you are early you can prepare yourself and be ahead of the curve.

Use Eye Contact and a Firm Handshake

Be prepared to meet the judges, and be enthusiastic. Look them in the eye and shake their hands firmly. (Mentors: it helps to demonstrate a firm handshake with the kids and let them practice.)

Give a Personal Greeting

If there are three or four judges sitting in a row within earshot of one another, be prepared to give different greetings as you go down the row to meet them. For example, when you hand a judge your business card and written materials, you might say:

- How do you do, my name is _____.
- So glad you could be here today, here are my materials.
- I hope you enjoy my presentation, thank you for coming today.
- I look forward to presenting and hearing your feedback.

2. During the Presentation

Nonverbal assessments are part of our culture and socialization. Often, we are not even aware we are making them. To that end, the judges are different from student peers. The judges are looking at a student presenter as a whole package, and part of their criteria for grading a student is the student's ability to give a convincing oral presentation.

The impression a student makes, whether confident and assured or disinterested and disorganized, comes through in his body language and words. People inherently sense whether a person believes what he is saying by his demeanor. This includes posture, body language, voice intonation, an internal belief that comes through words, and, of course, the ideas conveyed. This is a package that includes the following:

Good Posture

Remember to stand tall, shoulders back, head held high. (Demonstrate slouching and shuffling for your student to illustrate what not to do.)

Direct Eye Contact

Look around the audience as you convey your ideas. Make eye contact. Be aware of the level of audience interest. If the audience looks bored, change the cadence of your presentation, your physical movements, the volume of your voice, and/or your level of enthusiasm. Call on an audience member, ask a question, or demonstrate a point in your talk.

Movement

Some speakers like to walk around, point to things, hand out documents or samples, and basically keep the audience on their toes while speaking.

Voice Articulation and Messaging

People hear the tone of the voice, the melody of messages, as well as the volume. Speak slowly, and clearly. Use language that judges will understand. Often, there is a cultural or generational language gap that can hurt the presenter if judges do not understand a student's language. (I have witnessed this often!)

Key Points

When practicing with the three-by-five-inch flash cards, underline points of emphasis, and vary your vocalization. (A mentor might demonstrate what it sounds like to deliver a paragraph using a monotone; one using uptalk, with each declarative sentence ending in an up melody so that it sounds like a question; and a statement spoken with emphasis and conviction.)

Slang

Slang and filler words such as "umm," "like," "ya know," "kinda," and "sorta" can be humanizing when used occasionally, but are annoying when used repeatedly. Avoid using these, as well as slang words that are too informal for your presentation. (When students practice, it is helpful for mentors to make them aware of their verbal tendencies.)

Positivity

There are many ways to convey an idea. Consider negative wording: "I would never pick anything else, 'cause nothin' compares with . . . " versus positive wording: "It's been my experience that this is beneficial for many reasons."

Positive messaging comes across through action verbs and positive language, words such as: creative, design, demonstrate, believe, complete, envision, oversee, manage, direct, please, devise, impress, accomplish, and praise.

Often students lace their comments with "kinda" and "sorta," or speak within insecure, incomplete, or negative framing. A good exercise would be to have students take several ideas and construct positive and negative messaging so they understand the differences.

Smile

Share what you have enjoyed and explain how this was a stimulating process that piqued your curiosity.

3. Post-Presentation

At the close of the presentation, judges will usually ask questions. As a mentor, you should listen to your mentees with a critical ear and try to prepare them for the kinds of questions you yourself would ask. Play devil's advocate and ask the tough questions. It is better to give the mentee good practice and have the experience of responding while on his feet than to have him surprised on the day of the presentation. I find that questions fall into one of the categories below. Of course, myriad potential answers may be given, but advise your student to be deferential, accurate, respectful, and attentive. A mindset of openness rather than defensiveness is helpful. Remind the mentee that, though she has worked on this material for a long time, the audience is hearing it for the first time. They are learners. Patience and clarity are key.

The following are samples of good scripted responses by students:

Judge: *Suggestion*—"You might consider looking at it this way. In my experience . . . "

Student: "I hadn't thought of that, thank you for your input." "I was considering this as an idea, but couldn't pursue it because of limitations."

Judge: *Clarification*—"The research on the fourth slide wasn't clear to me. Can you clarify?"

Student: "I'm so glad you asked that, let me refer back to this slide." "Let me further explain . . . does this answer your question adequately?"

Judge: *Objection*—"It's never been my understanding that this is how it worked. In fact, I have found it works differently than you described."

Student: "Yes, I appreciate your comment, and I considered this when I was doing my research. I may not have dedicated enough time to this issue. Thank you for bringing it to my attention, let me explain my findings further."

Short Group Exercises

Handshake

Demonstrate with one student a shy, reticent, limp handshake, without making eye contact. Then demonstrate a different posture, with a smile, a forward comment, and direct eye contact. Ask students to respond to the differences in the two characters you demonstrated.

Have students turn to each other and enact both the behavior you demonstrated. Ask them how each feels? Are they different? Do the students have suggestions? Allow them to discuss their reservations.

Body Language

Divide the class into three groups for a role-play exercise. Distribute the following instructions. Each group will develop a pitch from a unique perspective.

Pitch Story (for All Three Groups)

All three groups will work together to prepare a researched (or made up) two- to three-paragraph pitch about an exciting new form of low-calorie, super-creamy yogurt from Greece. This can be a competitive exercise if you decide. Students are trying to persuade two buyers from Whole Foods to sell their product in the stores. They need to try to understand what the priorities will be for the buyers. They need to have created background facts on their yogurt and its benefits, and they need to take on the perspective of the character they have been assigned to play. The objective is to piece all these elements together into a convincing public pitch with all the data points converged. It is a fun role-playing exercise, and good for discussion afterward.

Pass the following descriptions out to each group, and give them fifteen minutes to prepare and select a spokesperson. No groups know the others' assignment, so each will be seeing a completely different scenario. Also, remember to select two students to play buyers from Whole Foods.

Group One: Handout

Your spokesperson *has just arrived from Greece.* He is extremely shy, with a heavy accent, and has a long line of ancestors, some of whom developed a recipe for yogurt many decades ago. He or she should be shuffling, looking down at the floor, and be a little hard to hear but excited about Greek culture, the newness of this product to America, and how authentic the yogurt is to Greece.

Group Two: Handout

Your spokesperson is a *slick businessperson* who has invested in this yogurt company as well as in many other companies selling new-to-market food products. She or he knows that the market has a void in the creamy yogurt area, and with good posture, a firm voice, a confident stride, and assembled facts on demographics and price points (it is okay to make them up for this exercise) proves to buyers why they need to carry this product.

Group Three: Handout

Your spokesperson is from the distribution side of the business. He or she has a long-standing relationship with Whole Foods markets nationally, and throws this information around freely. He cares more about the relationship, as this is only one of many products he represents. This pitch is mostly about maintaining relationships, as well as about shelf life, practicality, and whether the product will sell based on price point. (You are welcome to make up data points for the purpose of the exercise.) You try to use familiarity and friendship to win the buyers over. You are less professional, might use a bit of slang, and could even playfully ignore a few of the buyers' questions to steer them toward how nicely this will fit next to other products you represent.

At the end of the three presentations, ask the groups to discuss the differences. Who would they buy from and why? What were their reactions to each? What are some of the takeaways? Write these on the board as students share. Ultimately, you want to bring the conversation around to the elements of a good presentation, what is believable, understanding your audience, and projecting your ideas with conviction.

Three to Five Ads

Over the course of a week, ask students to pay attention to advertisements on television, in the newspaper, on public transportation, and on billboards. They should find three to five different examples of ads that caught their attention and be prepared to explain why to the class.

Positive versus Negative Framing

Draw a line down the middle of a flip chart or board. Write "Positive" on one side of the line and "Negative" on the other. Ask the students to call out positive words and experiences that feel good. As they do, write them down. If they are not forthcoming, suggest experiences for them, such as "won a match," "got a good grade on a test," "received a compliment," phrases that feel positive.

Do the same with negative thoughts and experiences, keeping things clean! The point of this exercise is that we all have choices in the way we frame our thoughts and communicate them to others.

Ask half the group to write a three-sentence paragraph with positive terms describing any subject, for example, the school football team or food served in the cafeteria for lunch that day. Ask the other half to write a three-sentence paragraph with negative terms describing the same subject as the positive group.

Ask students to read their paragraphs aloud to demonstrate the difference positive and negative messaging can have on the presenter and on the way an audience perceives the content.

Presentation Summary

In closing this chapter on "The Art of Presenting," I have included the following presentation critiques for you to use when listening to and helping to prepare your mentee. Additionally, you will find a series of inspirational quotes to share with your mentee on the art of being authentic and persevering through adversity.

Style Critique

  1. *Voice*
     a. Pace
     b. Articulation

      c. Enthusiasm

      d. Physical presence

      e. Posture

      f. Gestures

      g. Movements

2. *Visuals*
   a. Readable
   b. Functional
   c. Consistent
   d. Value-added
   e. Entertaining
3. *Eye contact*
   a. Directed around room
4. *Language*
   a. Understandable
   b. Varied
   c. Uses active voice
   d. Positive

Organizational Critique

1. *Opening*
   a. Objective
   b. Clear (format)
   c. Logical
2. *Points*
   a. Examples are shown on creative slides
   b. Facts are accurate and researched
   c. Process is thorough and professional
3. *Conclusion*
   a. Brief and to the point
   b. Mirrors the objective
   c. Offers conclusive results

4. *Handling questions*
   a. Respectful
   b. Good grasp of content

Recap

If I were to be completely obnoxious (on rare occasions), out of the fifteen years Phil and I have been mentoring—our students have placed "first" in the region-wide competitions *eighteen* times. Go figure? I'm not a hundred percent certain what the secret sauce is for this track record beyond what I've already shared in this chapter, except that we have fun! We encourage students to trust themselves and their gut. We give them one-on-one time rehearsing presentations together. We remind them that their ideas are valuable and unique, and that the judges want to hear them. Inevitably we are present in the audience during their final performance, quietly cheering them on. I guarantee you, our mentees cannot wait to come up to us afterwards and hear our words of praise, especially after all we've been through together. That said, all the other mentors, parents, and teachers are standing on the sidelines too. It's at this moment I realize how right Hillary Clinton was, when she wrote, "It takes a village."

Note

1. Eric Liu, *Guiding Lights: How to Mentor and Find Life's Purpose* (New York: Ballantine Books, 2006), xii.

CHAPTER 11

BRINGING CLASS TO A CLOSE

What Happens to the Mentor–Mentee Relationship?

Patty, did you ever know, ten years ago, that you could change people's lives? I talk about spiritual genetics in my latest book; where each of us can choose the spirit of who you want to become. It has nothing to do with bloodlines. You have made a difference in the lives of these kids, and most likely you have made a difference in the lives of their kids as well. They have grabbed hold of your light, maybe because they had no other.

—Chris Gardner, author of *The Pursuit of Happyness*,
at the 2010 D.C. NFTE Gala

Living is about changing, even when we don't want change or don't trust it. Our educational challenge is built around these interventions and encounters. It is designed to shape unfolding changes so that a young person, hopefully, emerges with a widening array of choices and a capacity to think through them.

It's hard to believe that a short-term, limited connection can make much of a difference in this adventure toward maturation. But most of us still remember that visitor who came by the house, the stranger who made the important and unexpected observation (perhaps about us, perhaps about life in general, perhaps about both), or the individual who functioned as a sort of ambassador from a world that was, at the time, still very far away. The encounter may have been brief, but it opened a door. And if that stranger managed to speak to our own place of possibility, an inner dialogue began, and continued long after the memorable outsider moved on.

Mentors are those significant strangers. They offer themselves to encounters that may turn out to be transformative. The encounter, even if it continues for several months, is short in the context of a life, so any transformation is necessarily the result of a ripple effect or a movement along a new trajectory. The mentor essentially throws the pebble into the pond, and perhaps what begins is a first circle of many ripples. From there it's a matter of good choices and good luck, and then more good choices and more good luck—none of which a mentor can direct.

I didn't have a clue, when I met certain students between 2001 and 2015, what would follow. Nor could I even make a reasonable guess about which students might not, despite their various efforts, realize even a scaled-back version of their life dreams. When you enter a classroom on the first day and peer out into a sea of blank student faces, you take a risk. You don't know who is listening, and you certainly don't know *why*. What you notice is that some seem to be tuning in while others seem to be tuning out. You'll be granted some interesting signals, a few clues, and maybe even a minor revelation or two, but your students' unique and complex circumstances will be more or less mysterious to you, and they mostly will remain that way. You don't do this for the short term nor are you guaranteed a payoff. You know that every student can, in fact, do something new, something he hasn't done before, something he doubted he could ever do. That is what makes all the difference.

While you're with these students, the listening you do is of utmost importance, as is the patience required to assist change in another person whom we only partly understand. To understand "*the ripple*" you have to *wait and listen*, sometimes for years. Then you may see the ways your presence and your persistence made a life different. This virtuous cycle spirals back to you when you least expect it. When it arrives, you experience the privilege of sharing in a young person's hard-earned success. Yes, it's 100 percent the other person's success, but you glow with pride that your student's success is, in some small part, your success as well. To touch another life is the best, most enduring gift imaginable. But you won't know that you have done so, or how you have, for some time.

This chapter reflects my waiting and listening. I share with you the virtuous cycle and how it came to reveal itself to me. You can observe in our closing chapter a beautiful ripple that began with a well-designed and well-timed encounter in mentorship.

Where are my mentees today? How did they transition out of the school year? Did I maintain relationships? Are they forging entrepreneurial paths? Are they better prepared to enter the workforce than if Phil and I had not mentored them? Are they citizens of their communities, giving back and paying it forward?

I will share some best practices in bringing the relational arc to a gentle close or shift, and highlight what several students, among the six hundred-plus I have mentored, are doing years after our classroom encounters.

Setting Expectations for Closure

From the first day you enter class and outline your role as a mentor, you establish expectations and structure. You make it clear that your mentoring function parallels the curricular schedule. The project's body of work, concluding with an oral defense and summary, as well as a final grade, offers additional milestones toward closure between you and your students.

Because the mentoring relationship is unique, it can be difficult to transition. Sometimes a special friendship, even a dependency, shows itself. Some students may not even acknowledge appreciation of your attention, your guidance, or your support until much later in their lives. Based on what most students express at the time, a mentor has reason to wonder if the students experienced much of an impact at all. Then again, there are others who are abundantly grateful, so much so that they don't want to let go.

Soft Closures

First, let's look at designing soft closures that lend structure to the transition. As mentors, Phil and I have experimented with end-of-year moments. The following ideas have worked for us.

End-of-Year Meal

After the final presentations have been completed, we like to take the students and their teacher for a special meal, either lunch or breakfast. This is nothing fancy—we tend to choose whatever is nearby and convenient. Of course, it needs to fit with the students' schedule, and it is preferable to have table service and a reasonably quiet environment.

This occasion is a way of showing the students they are important, we have enjoyed working together, we respect their commitment and effort, we celebrate the close of the year, and we are delighted to be their hosts. For many, being taken for a meal is a truly special treat outside of the ordinary.

At the start of the meal, the mentor typically shares a year-end review that expresses feelings and recollections. I like to say: "We just want to say how much we have enjoyed coming to your class and getting to know each and every one of you. It has been remarkable to witness how far you have come since our first one-on-one meetings. We have made huge strides together. We would like to point out a couple of outstanding examples." Remind them of several comic or significant examples that the whole class would remember.

"Finally, we want to thank (Mr./Ms. Teacher), not only for putting up with us, but for giving us guidance and for his immense talents as an educator. Can we give him a round of applause?" Sometimes we bring a token gift for the teacher to open in front of the class.

Then, I hand out one four-by-six-inch index card with several questions printed on it. We ask each student to stand, answer the questions, and be true to her heart; we tell them that we care about their input and really want to hear what each has to say. Sample questions follow:

- What were your three biggest takeaways from this year's class?
- In hindsight, what was your biggest hurdle with your project? How did you overcome it?
- How would you describe the class to students who were curious about your experience?
- How can we improve as mentors?

It may be an unprecedented experience for certain students to be asked what they think of work that adults have led. Your asking reinforces the message that you respect their insights and opinions.

The meal gets us out of our standard workaday mode and allows us to connect as *people* enjoying one another. Shifting from working together to dining together is common in the business world. Often, employees break bread together to celebrate the end of a big project. This mimics that pattern of professional life.

Additionally, students observe how we conduct ourselves in a restaurant, our table manners, and our interactions with staff. Most importantly, it's the last event before we disperse. The meal hopefully leaves all of us with positive feelings, as well as a shared understanding that the process we've embarked on together is coming to a conclusion.

Year-End Appreciation Book

As part of the *Teach to Work* approach, we urge each teacher who has enjoyed the participation of mentors to assemble a three-ring binder (for each mentor) that commemorates the year, particularly if the mentor has been an underwriter of the class. I am the proud owner of fifteen binders filled with field trip photos, articles from high school newspapers and local business journals, chamber of commerce awards, thoughtful letters of appreciation from students, and samples of year-end presentations. (Many of the excerpts in this book are taken from these correspondences.)

As a mentor, the Appreciation Book means the world to me. It reflects students' thoughts about the content and effort you have shared. As part of the rite of passage, the book is usually presented by the teacher, ceremonially, at the year-end lunch.

Between you and me, I can hardly wait to spend an afternoon curled up under a blanket, slowly combing through each and every word, taking in the ways that I somehow made a real difference for so many students. These letters provided the impetus for this book and for my request that you consider sharing your knowledge and experience as well. Perhaps the most significant letter comes from a student I know the least, a boy or girl who has seemed withdrawn, reticent, perhaps even completely tuned out, but who was nonetheless touched significantly by a sentence, a gesture, or a small effort on my part. You can't know what seeds you might be planting, just by being there. Nor do you have to wait until you are sure you're capable of doing something heroic. Start by showing up—it goes further than you might think.

Teachers often suggest students consider some of the following thoughts for their letters:

- What have you learned from one-on-one sessions? Focus on a particular session, if possible.
- How and why are you grateful—for your mentor's time, knowledge, or contribution?
- What do you anticipate doing with your newfound knowledge?
- What plans do you have for the future?

Learning to write a thank-you note and show appreciation for another's time, knowledge, and gift of support is mandatory in the world of business. Students should learn this in school, as they may not be learning professional etiquette in other contexts.

Some teachers have elicited thank-you notes from the students after each activity the mentor has led all year long. Whether it's bringing guest speakers, leading a special-interest class, sending students on a field trip, or working one on one, there is a student letter for each activity.

Same Time Next Year

If you are considering continuing as a mentor at the same school the following year, invite your mentees to stop by to visit you and share their latest endeavors and successes. When you work with freshman and sophomores, there is a strong likelihood you will run into your former mentees in the hallways the following year. This is a great moment to catch up, or invite the student back for an after-class visit.

It is also possible to coordinate with the teacher and have the previous year's mentees return to address the current class. We have interviewed past students, in a talk show format, about their memories of the class and the best practices they took away. The current class observes the ease and familiarity you enjoy with their upperclassmen and graduates, which paves the way for their relationship with you ("Look how well they get along and like each other, maybe I *will* give this mentor a chance!").

This encounter with last year's mentee is another way to maintain an informal, ongoing connection through the auspices of the school.

Special Interest Club, Benefactor, or Speaker

Depending on your expertise, you could offer to return to a particular school club where you might guest speak, meet the club coordinator, and participate with some of your past mentees on an ongoing basis, after school. It expands the relationship when you make yourself available for an activity that didn't originate with you.

Nonprofit Affiliation

As mentioned, I came to mentoring through the Network for Teaching Entrepreneurship, a nonprofit that was already part of the public school system. The Network for Teaching Entrepreneurship is exactly that—a network! Students are invited back for various events, whether it's to get more education, attend alumni gatherings, compete at a higher level, serve as a guest speaker, participate in a marketplace to demonstrate and sell their product, volunteer for the organization, or just learn how to network with adults. For me, as the mentor, it's an easy and natural way to keep up with students who participate in the NFTE network, as well.

The point is that, as a mentor, reconnecting with your mentees through an *established framework* makes continuing any relationship quite easy and appropriate. This holds true for virtual connections as well. If a student asks for additional advice or input after the formal mentoring relationship concluded, I typically copy others on my e-mail correspondence; that is, I include my NFTE representative, the teacher, and my co-mentor.

Boundaries Broken

Embarking on a one-on-one mentor–mentee relationship on your own, particularly when your mentees are underage, **is not advisable**. If you wanted to continue to meet with the mentee, I would recommend doing so through the auspices of the nonprofit or the school by using their events and locations to reconnect. These gestures serve to honor important boundaries that can be tested and challenged with students.

Mentor Transitions

That said, once students are adults, you are on your own with where you take that friendship. Even then, there are often complex questions about whether and how you might share professional networks or financial resources with a former mentee, whose contacts and finances are likely to be limited.

I want to share several scenarios of post-school relationships and how I have conducted myself as a former mentor. You will recognize many of the students you have already heard about, as they enter their twenties and thirties. Rodney, an exceptional young man, is the only one I will introduce for the first time.

Rodney: A Story of Transformation

I never actually mentored Rodney in a classroom, per se. We created a mentor–mentee relationship, however, that has stood the test of time—seven years and counting.

Rodney and I first met in July 2009 in Aspen, Colorado. He was nineteen years old, stood about six foot, two inches, and was bean-pole thin, African

American, and obviously uncomfortable standing among the affluent, 99 percent Caucasian population gathered on the lawn of the Aspen Institute.

You see, Rodney was invited to be a guest speaker that evening following the airing of a new film—*Ten9Eight*—in which he was not only featured but served as the narrator. Through Mary Mazzio's brilliant direction, the film traced twelve of NFTE's entrepreneur students from all over the country leading up to and through the finals of the National Business Plan Competition in New York. Rodney was featured because he had won the regional business plan competition in Chicago.

As a NFTE board member, I had seen the film and had been instrumental in having it featured at the Aspen Institute's Ideas Festival. I was a hostess for the preview event and knew who Rodney was, but he didn't know me from Adam.

While everyone around him was hobnobbing with bigwigs, it looked like this young man could use a friend. So I approached him and introduced myself, "Welcome, Rodney, I'm Patty, also from NFTE. Tell me, have you ever been to Colorado before?" He willingly shared, "Not only have I never been to Colorado, this is my first time traveling outside of Chicago, I've never been on an airplane, nor have I ever seen a mountain. All of this is totally new." I replied excitedly, "Well, then, do I have something to show you—follow me." I walked three minutes away as he trailed my steps, a calculated break from all the people and hubbub. We arrived upon a quiet, magnificent meadow right on the institute's campus with a spectacular three-hundred-and sixty-degree view. We were surrounded by snow-capped mountains, an immense skyline streaked by the brilliant orange sunset, and prickly sagebrush at our feet. Rodney took it all in. He rotated in a slow circle. His eyes were wide open. His chest filled as he drew in a large deep breath of fresh air. He was awestruck. I surmised that this was a marked contrast from the noise and clutter of Chicago's urban streets. It was at this moment that Rodney and I connected, and I believe he knew I was a person he could trust. "Rodney," I said, "It's one thing to see mountains from afar, it's quite another to traverse them up close—I wonder if a city boy can make it up a mountain? In the next few days, if you can take it," I said with a little friendly goading, "we are definitely going to go for a hike while you are here."

The feature film aired a few minutes later at Paepcke Auditorium, where all four hundred attendees learned Rodney's backstory.

Since he was five years old, Rodney had been in thirteen foster-care homes. His dad had suffered from post-traumatic stress after Vietnam and turned to drug abuse as his coping mechanism. His subsequent financial demise devastated the family. Rodney and six of his brothers and sisters were placed in foster care, scattered throughout the city. Not only did they lose the possibility of sibling support because of geographic separation, but at young ages several brothers were already getting drawn into various forms of juvenile delinquency.

Rodney ran away. At seventeen, he checked out of foster care and into a homeless shelter from which he was ejected by six o'clock each morning. He would quickly take a sponge bath in the school bathroom before attending his first class. No one knew of his circumstances. It is understandable that Rodney had a hard time maintaining even a 1.3 grade point average. But eventually, at the start of his senior year, something changed for Rodney, and it set him on a new trajectory.

In 2007, he enrolled in the school's entrepreneurship class for the sole purpose of winning the $300 award money for the in-class competition. Most importantly, at the same time he met a mentor, whom I do not know, but who helped him shift his perspective dramatically. With the support of the mentor and the NFTE team, Rodney won the business plan competition by creating the plan for a video production company. He had turned a corner. By his senior year, his grade point average rose dramatically, to 3.5.

Fast-forward several months and Rodney was caught up in a whirlwind. He was invited by NFTE to New York City to compete nationally. He placed second in the NFTE national competition. His life story was featured among the dozen other students in the film *Ten9Eight*. His voice was chosen to narrate the film. And, he was invited to Aspen for the film preview.

By the summer of 2009 when we met, he had just completed his first year of college at Morehouse in Atlanta, Georgia. Rodney was accustomed to living life hand to mouth, never quite knowing how he would get by even a few days into the future. (This always struck me with horror, but it was his reality.) He scraped by, funding his first year with his $5,000 winnings (from taking second place in the NFTE competition) and a student loan. But he had no idea where the rest of his tuition would come from for the balance of his education, which he desperately wanted to continue.

When the film ended that night, Rodney walked onstage to a standing ovation. There was not a dry eye in the house. Even Tom Friedman was moved. He wrote a column in the *New York Times* titled "More (Steve) Jobs, Jobs, Jobs, Jobs," inspired by the documentary, which said, "Obama should arrange for this movie to be shown in every classroom in America. It is the most inspirational, heartwarming film you will ever see."[1]

The next evening, after the promised mountain hike, I hosted Rodney and a few others, including the movie producer, the NFTE CEO, a VP from the Aspen Institute, and a close friend, for a casual Italian dinner. During dinner, my dear friend leaned over to me and whispered, "I would like to help Rodney finish college." This was a rare moment—a confluence of events that you can never plan.

I suggested that she tell him her idea herself. Rodney was sitting directly across the table from us quietly eating his spaghetti when she said, "Rodney, I've decided I would like to help you finish your education at Morehouse College." He dropped his fork. There was a prolonged silence; he was practically speechless. He softly uttered, "What? Are you serious? That would be incredible!" She offered some boundaries saying, "You know, Rodney, you will have to hold up your end of the bargain—it's important for you to know that you would be required to maintain a grade point average, but I've been so impressed with you, I would really like to help you." At that moment, we all witnessed a life changed.

Those of us at that dinner have been tracking Rodney ever since, and his trajectory has continued to be more than remarkable. As of this writing:

- Rodney graduated with honors from his class at Morehouse in four years.
- He earned a Master of Divinity from Yale Divinity School.
- Rodney is working on a second master's degree in business from Yale.

- Rodney has published a book about his journey.
- He has decided he wants to pursue a PhD in education.

To this day, Rodney contacts me when he is in Washington. Sometimes, I think he even makes a special trip if he's feeling lonely or lost. Over the course of these seven years, we have seen each other two or three times a year, either at NFTE events or just for a conversation. While this is not a traditional Project Based Mentoring relationship, I believe Rodney stays in touch because he knows I care, will offer constructive feedback and help him brainstorm his ideas, and may even make more introductions on his behalf. He knows that I "have his back" and am trustworthy.

As a matter of fact, I flew to Yale to watch him graduate. It was a defining moment for me as a mentor and for all students who have come from backgrounds like Rodney's.

In my heart, I believe Rodney's success stems from his ability to survive and to invite mentorship into his life. He has sought out role models to emulate. He was willing to work, if only given the chance. He has tapped into the NFTE network extensively, finding internships, jobs, and advisors across the country (Goldman Sachs and MasterCard, particularly). He is also excellent at following up on leads. I am only one of his many mentors, and a proud one at that.

Because Rodney has excelled beyond his own wildest dreams, I believe he wants to pay it forward, not only by educating students but by sharing his story to inspire others. He certainly has inspired me. His new book is titled *A New Day One: Trauma, Grace, and a Young Man's Journey from Foster Care to Yale.*

Rodney was inspired by this quote by Maria Robinson, in *From Birth to One*: "Nobody can go back and start a new beginning, but anyone can start today and make a new ending."

Andre: A Story of Resourcefulness

You first met Andre in chapter 2. In high school he had a business called *Break Yo Neck Kicks*, which sold remnant Air Jordan tennis shoes. He found them online at big discount prices, created a brochure to market them to high school students, and developed a network of salespeople at other high schools to take orders and receive commissions. Andre has never been one to take shortcuts; rather, it is his nature to delve in tenaciously and go the distance.

Like Rodney, Andre has grown adept at cultivating mentors. He has extracted knowledge and support from many of our D.C. board members, whether for internships, introductions, letters of recommendation, or advice. It is an incredible takeaway for students to understand their own strengths, but also to identify their weaknesses. Learning how to be resourceful and who to go to for what—while garnering useful knowledge or practical skills—is a valuable mentoring outcome.

To date, Andre, twenty-eight, is poised to open his first pilot restaurant. His lease is signed, renderings are in progress, and construction pricing is in step. Half Smoke is opening in Shaw, an up-and-coming, gentrified area of Washington, D.C. Andre has written what some have said is the best business plan they have ever seen, complete with projections, competitive menus, vision thinking, timelines, and voids in the marketplace—all presented with high-end graphics. Impressive. Since high school, Andre's analytic mind and curiosity landed him in a series of growth jobs, including at UBS and JBG. What's more, in his spare time on weekends, he would leave his high-paying Wall Street job and work as a prep chef in progressive concept kitchens throughout D.C., travelling back and forth to New York weekly. He has gone the distance, finding a cadre of renowned foodie experts who serve on his advisory council. He has tapped friends and family as his first-round investors. I can share that Andre has visions of scaling his new idea nationally. I believe from his behavior and commitment that he *will* be the next Chipotle for the sausage industry. I am not alone. Members of the D.C. board of NFTE are all there cheering him on every inch of the way.

Phil and I were Andre's first NFTE mentors when he was sixteen years old, and he has reached out whether he has been in New York, London, or back home in D.C. To this day, he still checks in with me, whether it is for menus to review, tastings, design plans, construction projections, concept schemes, public relations introductions, or just marketing ideas. He contacts

Phil for financial analysis, lending scenarios, strategic management choices, or hiring decisions. Just by observing his sourcing methods, you understand his depth of thinking. You could say he has our numbers.

In regard to Andre as a community-minded person, I am proud to say he single-handedly spearheaded the NFTE Leadership Council for Young Entrepreneurs under the age of thirty-five. He built a robust team of twenty-five advisors and taught them about giving back. Andre is always available to speak to NFTE classes, sharing his knowledge with the next generation. He holds dear his D.C. roots, which are front and center conceptually for his new venture. When I asked if he would prefer to own a national chain outright, or consider franchising, his first inclination was toward a franchise model for the sole reason that he could create jobs and entrepreneurship opportunities for others.

At the 2015 NFTE gala, Andre was presented as the Locally Grown Honoree. I had the privilege of sitting next to his mother as he spoke from the lectern. Andre's voice cracked a little when he shared this tale: "Ya know my mother is a native Washingtonian. She grew up in Shaw, the exact same neighborhood of D.C. where I will soon open my new restaurant. However, times were different then. It was her experience, walking up this very street in the late fifties, that not a single restaurant door was open to her. She experienced the pains of racism on a daily basis." He then turned to his mother eye to eye and said, "So, Mom, as long as I am here, there will ALWAYS be a seat for you at my restaurant. You can count on that." His Mom quietly gestured, moving her hand to touch her heart.

Stay tuned, as you will be hearing much more about this young man in the future.

Khaled: Inspiring Cookie Man

Remember the 106-calorie Delicious New York Honey-Made Cookies developed by this remarkable fourteen-year-old student? You met Khaled in the introduction. He came to class and was certain he did not have the least bit of interest in business. For this reason, I find his story compelling, particularly after learning of his journey.

Remember that he won the in-class competition, the regional competition, and placed fifth nationally. He rented out Harris Teeter's commercial kitchen, and sold his healthy brand of cookies at Target, Giant Food, and Harris Teeter, selling approximately thirty-two thousand cookies from the time he was fourteen until he was sixteen. Whew!

We have been in touch in a variety of ways. Khaled comes to class as a guest speaker when he is in town. He attends NFTE events and has been an honoree, so we catch up there. Also, we e-mail each other to learn of updates, progress, and life. He requested that I write a letter of reference for college admission. Most recently he shared with me what he is doing:

> Patty, over the summer the cookie business was going great, selling online and shipping. I overcame the problem of cookies breaking after a few changes. I've decided to only ship cookies during my summers from college, till I have more time to commit.
>
> In August I started classes at Clark, studying economics and entrepreneurship. I work as the project coordinator for the Innovation and Entrepreneurship program. I chair the Venture Committee, which oversees all student-run ventures on campus, evaluating performance and determining whether they should receive funding. However, the most exciting news is I will be working with the director of the Innovation and Entrepreneurship Program for NFTE mentorships in our local high schools. I will be coaching students with business plans and recruiting mentors. Lastly, my biggest project is the Eureka Big Ideas Challenge. Students submit ideas through a long application process that focuses on challenges for getting their idea off the ground. After five months of coaching they pitch ideas for a $5,000 award.
>
> As for my master plan, I am learning a lot and building connections. In the spring, I will be giving Harvard and Babson a try to transfer to a new school.

This summer I will work on marketing and branding my cookies and diversifying into different products, maybe selling at farmers markets and shipping only. . . .

If any of the above sounds a tiny bit interesting, please know that YOU made it happen. I often think about how just the thought of being where I am today was unbelievable five years ago. I am grateful beyond words for your continuous support!

Thank you,
Khaled

The IT Gal

Chante started at Suitland High as a jock. Her first love at the time was basketball, so when she entered business she wasn't clear about her intentions. She did share with us that there was a secret inclination toward computers, and of course we explored this notion and encouraged it. But she was never one to need much prodding. As a matter of fact, I'd have to say, I have never seen any student delve in head first and be so utterly consumed by their business as Chante was.

Then I learned a little about Chante's home life. When she was twelve years old, her mother died. Her ten-year-old sister and eight-year-old brother looked to her as the oldest, for guidance and support. At that tender age not only did Chante have to mature quickly, but she made every effort to hide her pain and protect her siblings from more heartache. Working alongside her elderly grandmother, Chante took on more and more responsibilities. In her mind, she wanted to set a good example, work hard at school, get good grades, and demonstrate discipline, all the while remembering her siblings on holidays, purchasing gifts, and being a source of constant support. At twelve, she was already toeing the line.

I would be negligent if I did not mention Ms. Mena Lofland, who was a leader in entrepreneurship education and an inspiration both as a disciplinarian and a motivator. Between her awesome teacher and her mentors,

Chante built strong role models and cheerleaders. In business, she went the extra mile learning every detail not only about computers, but about customer service, marketing, and delivery. Conscientious with a capital C.

Chante's business at the time was called Your Way Computer Services; she would provide home repair for the novice computer owner. As a mentor, standing on the sidelines, I never cease to be amazed at the metamorphosis of students like Chante. When we met, she was a shy female athlete. Inside of one year she transformed into a CEO. She grew to be a driven, happy, proud, and confident business woman. She learned skills for how to interact with people of all ages; her business was profitable; and her very countenance, posture, and interactions changed. I credit NFTE for this transformative education that is so needed for youth today.

I digress; back to Chante. She won the region-wide business plan competition *hands down*. Her presentation and collateral materials were beyond exemplary. She crushed all of her competitors. Between her extensive handouts, detailed service offerings, variances in pricing, demonstrated track record with recurring clients, marketing incentive packages, and an online presence, it was evident that she was motivated and succeeding. At sixteen years old, Chante was fully operational, and she has not stopped since.

I have witnessed this young lady's growth for ten years. I will never forget many of our encounters; however, the one that stands out most for me was when she approached me at a NFTE event in 2013, several years after she graduated from high school and from George Washington University, where she earned a degree in Management Information Systems. With her head held high and her voice confident, she said, "Guess what, Miss Patty? I have lots of big news to share with you. I now have five employees who I provide health-care for, and, I just bought my own three bedroom townhouse. It's been a big year!" You see, Chante had grown her business doing IT government contracting, either directly or as a sub-contractor from another one of her NFTE mentors (see chapter 2, Antwanye Ford). But what is so interesting to me is *what* she chose to share. She could have focused on her volume of business, her pre-eminent clients, the price of her home, or its location—instead Chante was proud to be a responsible employer. She was a leader that took care of others. And . . . she reached a milestone of the American Dream—she had purchased her own home.

Her achievements have continued consistently. She won the 2009 Growing Up CEO award given by the Initiative for a Competitive Inner City Top 100 Business gala; she was the youngest speaker at *Inc.* magazine's 500 annual conference; she was also a 2009 East Coast Regional Finalist in the Global Student Entrepreneurship Awards with NFTE, where the next day she presented her business plan before the New York Stock Exchange. Her continuing education has included ITIL v3 certification, and ISO 20000 and 27001 certifications. She has successfully run her business for ten years.

It won't surprise you that I see her often, because she is the youngest board member for the D.C.-Baltimore region of NFTE and she brings many valuable perspectives to the table. In her own words, she reflected, "If I could overcome losing my mother at age twelve, I could overcome anything. Now I can't wait to teach my brother and sister what I have learned." In my book, Chante is the 'it' girl!

Bruce and Glen: The Fashion Preachers Story

In chapter 10 you met Bruce and Glen, who, after getting feedback on their poor effort on their presentation, said, "Okay, okay, we will *slap some cheese on it*," meaning they would try harder. The brothers would be the first to say they have a twin thing, with tons of personality, daring fashion sense, and unstoppable creative artistic talent. We met at our first class in 2001. Their business, called Twin Sports, produced unisex designer headbands with urban slang printed in glitter. They earned $10,000 in two years at $4 a band. They bought their own clothes during their junior and senior years of high school and paid a portion of their first year's tuition and worked to pay other expenses at their design-oriented college.

Now in their late twenties and living in Manhattan, the twins have remained connected at the hip, taking on every opportunity together. Their careers have followed a parallel path in both leadership and fashion.

The quick update: Bruce and Glen went through two years of college and got paid internships in fashion design at the House of Deréon—Beyoncé's company. They decided to stop school because they couldn't afford it, and immediately moved to Manhattan after accepting joint positions in design and packaging. Since then, they have created many opportunities for themselves as women's fashion designers, working with American Rag and as lead women's designers for Sean "P. Diddy" Combs. Ultimately, they started their own accessory business in leather goods. They make handbags, gloves, and fantastic slap bracelets in a multitude of colors and with decorative jewels. I attended one of their many trunk shows at Henri Bendel's. Bruce and Glen have been at numerous NFTE events, not only to sell their products but as featured speakers. They never say no. This is often where we would meet after they first moved away. Not shy and retiring, the young men have become celebrity fashion police on social media during New York's fashion week.

They keep me in the loop, sending me links to their blog, YouTube feed, and Instagram photos. It seems there is always a prospect for new and exciting opportunities waiting at their door.

They have been true to their passions—fashion, design, and drawing. They are also, however, pulled by other talents—their magnetic personalities, showmanship, leadership, and spirituality. They are not only designing for outer beauty, they are designing for inner beauty too. "Fashion Preachers" is not a name I made up!

For the last ten years, the twins have led a ministry and have developed a following of more than four hundred congregants made up of Broadway actors and fashion models who worship at the Rock Church. Bruce and Glen lead Bible study classes during the week and on Sundays preach either at the Apollo Theater or in vacant TV studios. The Rock Church is the umbrella organization that has become their home away from home.

When I walked into a Sunday worship service and saw them in front of all those beautiful people, Glen caught my eye and paused—he put his hand to his heart. Then he proceeded to introduce me to the congregation as one of his early business mentors. He paused to do this between his dancing, singing, and sermonizing. I had to see the twins' leadership in action for myself. I had heard so much about it and how much it meant to them.

Since their mother passed away, I confess, I make a special effort to stay in touch. I take them to lunch or dinner whenever I am in New York, and I have introduced them to my husband and stepkids, either at NFTE events or when we are in Manhattan. And if they are available for Christmas or Thanksgiving, I have extended an invitation.

The Proud Mentor

Many students I have not yet mentioned whom I see or connect with through social media include Andrea, Dexter, Ken E., Jabious, Anthony, Jada, Robert, Sekeithia, Tatiana, Tia, and Clarence. There are many others with whom I have lost touch. It is interesting that out of hundreds of students, only a dozen or so stay connected. Each and every mentee I have had the pleasure of coaching has been a gift. Maybe this book will reconnect us in some way, or possibly show them a mentor's point of view and even inspire them to mentor others.

You can see that Rodney, Andre, Khaled, Chante, Bruce, and Glen have all taken entrepreneurial chances; are designing their futures; have gained confidence in themselves; have demonstrated that they have real grit, commitment, and follow-through; have developed robust support systems; and, interestingly, have given back to the communities where they reside. I could not be prouder to know them or to share their unique accomplishments. I can hardly wait to hear about the next steps of their journeys.

Teach to Work is all about building a corps of professionals and encouraging them to share their knowledge. It is much more than an idea; it is an action plan. The book gives you hands-on guidance for building your mentor–mentee relationship. It lays out a chronology of interactions from entering school and learning the rules of engagement to meeting the teacher to meeting the class to working one on one with individual students to collaborating on a student project and defending it.

Recap

As you have read, we are simply integrating a professional, a student, and a project into a working formula. We spell out how *your* expertise, *your* knowledge, and *your* abilities can, in fact, better prepare the next generation of students for the twenty-first-century workforce one student at a time. And, in the process, you might even motivate them to be good citizens too.

Discussions about the challenges of education tend to leave people overwhelmed. But what Rodney, Khaled, Andre, Chante, Bruce, Glen, and dozens of others are telling us is that student failure is *not* inevitable. Our young people are an extraordinary resource that deserves every investment. Youth are geniuses at improvisation and imagining what isn't obvious. Their powers of reinvention often far surpass even their own expectations, if they are given an invitation to succeed and the support and guidance of an interested adult.

Teach to Work has laid out the why and the how of mentoring, and the obvious next question is: where? I truly hope that my stories and writings will be a call to action for you.

Please see the next section, "Call to Action: Mentors' Resource Guide," for opportunities across the nation.

Note

1. Tom Friedman, "More (Steve) Jobs, Jobs, Jobs, Jobs," *New York Times*, January 23, 2010.

APPENDIX

A Call to Action: Mentors' Resource Guide

Finding a Mentoring Organization to Fit Your Needs

Many organizations engage mentors and would welcome your participation. The Mentors' Resource Guide is one of the most comprehensive guides available to help you find a place to lend your knowledge and skills. It is unique because it is divided by the mentor's industry or discipline.

Additions and addendums to the guide will be available on our website at www.teachtowork.com under the Resource tab. As well, if you are a multi-state nonprofit that seeks skills based mentors and are interested in inclusion, please contact us at info@teachtowork.com)

- Among your options, **nonprofit** education organizations such as NFTE, Junior Achievement, Decca, and NAF provide educational programming within schools as outside vendors. They act as a conduit between the mentor, the school, and the teacher of the subject. They establish background checks and offer training, guidelines, and continued mentor support. Contact information follows, categorized by mentor profession.
- Several **project based learning organizations** are listed in this guide too. Some offer mentorship placement as well as guidance on sourcing materials.

- Some **schools** provide mentoring roles, such as Citizen Schools, Expeditionary Learning, and Communities in Schools. They might be part of the education reform movement, who are providing creative, wider ranging programs that integrate community members and mentors. Additionally, school guidance counselors or development officers can either guide you to the nonprofits that are already in their schools or offer their own career academies or technical education programs for mentorship. It is important to know who to ask for and what to say to streamline your quest.
- **Community colleges** are adept at integrating business partners as adjuncts in their classrooms.
- **National community organizations**, including 4-H National Mentoring and Big Brothers Big Sisters, offer mentoring as one aspect of their community programming and might sponsor after-school projects that link corporations with needy students.
- Last, **national umbrella organizations**, including Achieve, Points of Light, America's Promise Alliance, Mentoring Partnerships, and the Corporation for National & Community Service, are national in scope and are establishing partnerships around mentoring geared toward alleviating poverty.

How to Use This Resource Guide

The resources presented below are a starting point that will help you find the best way to use your expertise to help a child learn and grow. While there are thousands of programs nationwide that seek adult mentors for children and teens, the organizations listed in this index are generally larger, operate in more than one state—in many cases, they operate nationwide—and tend to use adult mentors to help youth develop career-building skills or prepare youth for a specific career path. Mentors in these programs do not focus on helping children with emotional skill building as an adult might be expected to do in an organization like Big Brothers, Big Sisters. Readers wishing to serve as that type of mentor should visit the section "Online Clearinghouses" to learn more about web-based resources that list volunteer opportunities at the city, county, or state level.

Readers interested in mentoring youth, especially those interested in introducing teens and young adults to a particular profession, can use the information below to research available programs seeking adult mentors. It has been divided into sections to aid you in your search, including:

- **Industry-focused mentoring:** organizations and programs that seek mentors and role models from specific professional fields
- **Broad-based mentoring:** organizations and programs that seek adult role models to more broadly prepare youth for careers
- **Mentoring focused on career prep:** organizations and programs that seek mentors to help prepare youth for specific professional careers
- **Mentoring focused on college prep:** organizations and programs that seek mentors to help prepare youth for entrance into an institution of higher education
- **Mentoring through on-site apprenticeships:** organizations and programs that seek to link mentors and onsite apprenticeships to older students (high school and post high school)
- **Schools that use mentoring:** school networks that have altered the traditional K–12 curriculum to focus more on career exploration, skill building, experiential learning, and career prep
- **Online clearinghouses:** web-based resources that collect and list volunteer opportunities at the city, county, or state level

Industry-Focused Mentoring

Use this section to locate a mentoring opportunity by industry focus. It is organized first by the industry represented and then alphabetically by the name of the nonprofit organization seeking adult mentors.

Chart A.1 Industry-Focused Mentoring

Industry Represented	Name	Student-Focused Program	Sites/Locations	Ages Served	Website	Mailing Address of HQ	Phone/Electronic Contact
Architecture, Construction, and Engineering	ACE Mentor Program of America, Inc.	The ACE program helps to mentor high school students and inspires them to pursue careers in design and construction.	Nationwide and Puerto Rico	Grades 9–12	www.acementor.org	6110 Executive Blvd., Ste. 612, Rockville, MD 20852	571–297–6869, info@acementors.org
Aerospace Engineering	Air Force Association	The CyberPatriot progam hosts the annual Natioanl Youth Cyber Defense Competition, during which student-led, adult-mentored teams design and build aerospace-related projects.	Nationwide in selected high schools	Grades 9–12	www.uscyberpatriot.org	1501 Lee Hwy, Arlington, VA 22209	877–885–5716, info@uscyberpatriot.org

Arts	826 National	826 centers offer a variety of programs that provide underresourced students, with opportunities to explore their creativity and improve their writing and presentation skills.	CA, IL, MA, MI, NY, WA, D.C.	Grades 6–12	826national.org	44 Gough St., Ste. 206, San Francisco, CA 94103	415–864–2093, information@ 826national.org
Arts	Community Arts Experience, Inc.	CAE provides experiential learning opportunities through arts, media, and technology.	GA, OH, PA, SC, D.C.	Grades 3–12	www.community artsexperience. com	50 Pearl Ave SE, Massillon, OH 44646	330–956–9188, info@CEAWW. org
Business/ Finance	Future Business Leaders of America	FBLA prepares students for careers in business and business-related fields.	Nationwide	Grades 6–12, college	www.fbla-pbl. org	1912 Association Dr, Reston, VA 20191–1591	703–860–3334, general@fbla. org
Business/ Finance	Genesys Works	Genesys Works provides at-risk high school teens with summer internships at Fortune 100 companies.	CA, IL, MN, TX	Grades 11–12	www.genesys works.org bayarea	14400 Memorial Dr, Ste. 200, Houston, TX 77079	713–337–0522, info@ba.genesys works.org

(Continued)

Chart A.1 (Continued)

Industry Represented	Name	Student-Focused Program	Sites/Locations	Ages Served	Website	Mailing Address of HQ	Phone/Electronic Contact
Business/ Finance	Invest in Girls	IIG teaches high school girls financial concepts and exposes them to professional role models and career paths in finance.	CT, MA, MD, PA	Grades 9–12	www.investgirls. org	125 Lake St., Sherborn, MA 01770	617–899–0504, ahoffman@ investgirls.org
Business/ Finance	Sponsors for Educational Opportunity	SEO offers support for minority youth interested in finance careers through its Scholars, Career, and Alternative Investment programs.	CA, NY	Grades 9–12	www.seo-usa. org	55 Exchange Place, New York, NY 10005	212–979–2040, altinvest@seo-usa.org
Business/ Marketing	DECA	DECA prepares emerging leaders and entrepreneurs for careers in marketing, finance, hospitality, and management.	Nationwide	Grades 9–12, college	www.deca.org	1908 Association Dr., Reston, VA 20191	703–860–5000, info@deca.org

	Organization	Description	Location	Grades	Website	Address	Contact
Civil Service	Blacks in Government	Through its FLAG program, BIG prepares African American youth for careers in civil service.	Nationwide via chapters	Grades 6–12	www.bignet.org	3005 Georgia Ave. NW, Washington, D.C. 20001–3807	202–667–3280, bignational@bignet.org
Civil Service	Federally Employed Women	FEW is an advocacy group for women employed by the federal government, and it offers a mentoring program to increase the number of women in civil service.	Nationwide via chapters	college	www.few.org	455 Massachusetts Ave. NW, #306, Washington, D.C. 20001	202–898–0994, few@few.org
Computer Science	Computer Clubhouse	Computer Clubhouse's after-school programs allow at-risk, inner-city youth to explore and become skilled in the use of technology.	AZ, CA, CO, FL, GA, IL, MA, MI, MN, NM, NY, OR, PA, TX, UT, VA, WA, D.C.	Grades K–12	www.computerclubhouse.org	Museum of Science Boston, 1 Science Park, Boston, MA 02114	email@computerclubhouse.org
Computer Science	Girls Who Code	GWC Clubs and the Summer Immersion program offer computer science education to encourage STEM careers for girls.	CA, FL, GA, IL, MA, MI, NJ, NY, TX, WA	Grades 6–12	girlswhocode.com	28 W. 23rd St., 4th Fl., New York, NY 10010	6246–629–9735, online contact form at website

(Continued)

Chart A.1 (Continued)

Industry Represented	Name	Student-Focused Program	Sites/Locations	Ages Served	Website	Mailing Address of HQ	Phone/Electronic Contact
Computer Science	Technology Education And Literacy in Schools	TEALS places IT professionals in schools to teach kids about computer science.	Partners with schools in AZ, CA, CO, FL, IL, IN, KY, MA, MI, MN, ND, NY, NC, OH, SC, TX, UT, VA, WA	Grades 9–12	www.tealsk12. org	Online only	Online contact form at website
Computer Science	The Creating IT Futures Foundation	CITF programs provide IT education, training, certification, and career support to at-risk, underrepresented minority students.	GA, IL, MN, NC, NE, NY, OH, PA, TX, D.C.	College	www.creating itfutures.org	3500 Lacey Rd., Ste. 100, Downers Grove, IL 60515	630–678–8300, info@creating ITfutures.org
Construction	Mentoring a Girl in Construction	Through its free summer camp, MAGIC offers girls hands-on training in basic construction skills.	Camp locations move depending on need, funds, and interest expressed	Grades 9–12	www.mentoring agirlin construction. com	276 Bill Robison Rd., Auburn, GA 30011	reneeeconner 2008@yahoo. com

Construction	National Construction Career Days	NCCD is a one-day event to encourage students to explore careers in the building and manufacturing trades.	Nationwide but organized by local partners	Grades 6–12, post high school	www.uritc.org/nccD.C.	NCCD, c/o URI Transportation Ctr., 75 Lower College Rd., Kingston, RI 02881	401–874–7075, see website for appropriate contact
Construction	YouthBuild USA	YouthBuild programs offer low-income youth the opportunity to earn GEDs or high school diplomas while building affordable housing and participating in leadership development activities.	Nationwide, D.C., the Virgin Islands	Post high school	youthbuild.org	58 Day St., Somerville, MA 02144	617–623–9900, info@youthbuild.org
Culinary	National Restaurant Association Educational Foundation	The NRAEF's Pro Start two-year program teaches culinary techniques and management skills through real-life experience and classroom activities.	Nationwide	Grades 9–12	www.nraef.org/prostart	2055 L St. NW, Washington, D.C. 20036	800–424–5156, to volunteer, visit: www.nraef.org/Get-Involved/Industry-Support

(Continued)

Chart A.1 (Continued)

Industry Represented	Name	Student-Focused Program	Sites/Locations	Ages Served	Website	Mailing Address of HQ	Phone/Electronic Contact
Engineering	National Society of Black Engineers	NSBE's Pre-College Initiative and Engineering Summer Camp introduce African American youth to engineering careers.	Nationwide via chapters	Grades K–12	www.nsbe.org	205 Daingerfield Rd., Alexandria, Virginia 22314	703–549–2207, info@nsbe.org
Engineering	Society of Women Engineers	SWE offers several outreach programs designed to give girls hands-on engineering experience.	Nationwide via chapters	Grades 6–12	societyofwomen engineers.swe.org	203 N La Salle St., Ste. 1675, Chicago, IL 60601	877–793–4636, hq@swe.org
Engineering, IT, and Math	Expanding Your Horizons Network	EYHN organizes day-long STEM conferences to introduce and empower girls to pursue STEM-related careers.	Nationwide	Grades 6–12	www.eyhn.org	5000 MacArthur Blvd., PMB 9968, Oakland, CA 94613	510.277.0190, info@expanding yourhorizons.org

Category	Organization	Description	States	Grades	Website	Address	Contact
Engineering, IT, and Math	Great Minds in STEM	GMiS's programs create awareness, supply resources, and provide access to STEM-career pathways for Hispanic youth.	AZ, CA, FL, LA, MA, MD, MI, NV, NY, OH, OK, RI, TX, WA, D.C.	Grades K–12	www.greatmindsinstem.org	602 Monterey Pass Rd., Monterey Park, CA 91754	323–262–0997, info@greatmindsinstem.org
Engineering, IT, and Math	Techbridge	Techbridge programs offer hands-on projects and encourage disadvantaged girls to pursue STEM careers.	CA, WA, D.C.	Grades 6–12	www.techbridgegirls.org	7700 Edgewater Dr, Ste. 519, Oakland, CA 94621	510–777–9170, info@techbridgegirls.com
Engineering, IT, and Math	Women In Technology	The Girls in Technology program increases awareness of and excitement for STEM careers through chapters, mentors, and community outreach.	VA, MD	Grades 4–12	www.womenintechnology.org/git	200 Little Falls Rd, Ste. 205, Falls Church, VA 22046	703–393–1044, staff@womenintechnology.org
Engineering/IT	Boosting Engineering, Science & Technology (BEST)	During the annual BEST Competition, mentor-led student teams compete to present group projects created through robotics design.	AL, AR, CT, CO, FL, GA, KS, MN, MS, ND, NM, OH, OK, PA, SD, TN, TX	Grades 6–12	best.eng.auburn.edu	P.O. Box 1024, Georgetown, TX 78627	469–630–2525, bestED@bestinc.org

(Continued)

Chart A.1 (Continued)

Industry Represented	Name	Student-Focused Program	Sites/Locations	Ages Served	Website	Mailing Address of HQ	Phone/Electronic Contact
Engineering/IT	Curiosity Hacked	Curiosity Hacked chapters introduce students to STEAM (science, technology, engineering, art, and math) subjects and help them gain hands-on skills.	CA, FL, IL, MA, MD, NM, NY, TN, PA, WA	Grades 1–8	www.curiosity hacked.org	Online contact form at website	info@ curiosityhacked. org
Engineering/IT	Maker Education Initiative	Mentors work with Young Makers clubs to help student groups build projects and compete at regional Maker meet-ups.	Nationwide via chapters	Grades 6–12	makered.org/ youngmakers	1001 42nd St., Ste. 230, Oakland, CA 94608	contact@ youngmakers. org.
Entrepreneurship	BUILD	BUILD uses entrepreneurship education to excite and propel at-risk, low-income students through high school to college success.	CA, MA, NY, D.C.	Grades 9–12	www.build.org	2385 Bay Rd., Redwood City, CA 94063	info@build.org

Category	Organization	Description	Coverage	Website	Grades	Address	Contact
Entrepreneurship	Junior Achievement	JA offers many programs to educate students about workforce readiness, entrepreneurship, and financial literacy.	Nationwide	www.juniorachievement.org	Grades K–12	One Education Way, Colorado Springs, CO 80906	719–540–8000, volunteer@ja.org
Entrepreneurship	Network for Teaching Entrepreneurship	NFTE provides programs that inspire low-income kids to stay in school, recognize business opportunities, and learn about entrepreneurship.	CA, FL, GA, IL, MA, MO, NY, PA, SC, TX, WA, D.C.	nfte.com	Grades 6–12	120 Wall St., 18th Fl., New York, NY 10005	212–232–3333, online contact form at website
Entrepreneurship	New Leaders Council	NLC trains and supports the next generation of progressive political entrepreneurs via training and mentorship.	CA, CO, CT, GA, FL, IA, IL, KY, LA, MD, ME, MI, MO, MT, NC, NE, NH, NJ, NY, OH, PA, RI, TN, WI, D.C.	www.newleaderscouncil.org	College	1200 New Hampshire Ave., NW, Ste. 575, Washington, D.C., 20036	202–885–9306, online contact form at website

(*Continued*)

Chart A.1 (Continued)

Industry Represented	Name	Student-Focused Program	Sites/Locations	Ages Served	Website	Mailing Address of HQ	Phone/Electronic Contact
Hospitality & Tourism	American Hotel & Lodging Educational Institute	The Hospitality High School Programs educate students about the skills needed to build a career in the hospitality and tourism industries.	Nationwide	Grades 9–12	www.ahlei.org	800 N. Magnolia Ave., Ste. 300, Orlando, FL 32803	407–999–8100, highschool@ahla.com
IT	Per Scholas	PS offers free, multi-week professional IT job training courses, career development, and job placement services to under-served communities.	GA, NY, OH, TX, D.C.	Post high school	www.perscholas.org	804 E. 138th St, 2nd Fl., Bronx, NY, 10454	718–991–8400, info@perscholar.org

IT	DigiGirlz High Tech Camp	Sponsored by Microsoft, the free DigiGirlz High Tech Camp is a two-day summer camp that allows young girls to explore careers in high tech, participate in hands-on workshops, and meet mentors.	MO, NC, ND, NV, TX, UT, WA	Girls only, grades 9–12	www.microsoft.com/en-us/diversity/programs/digigirlz/default.aspx	msgirlz@microsoft.com
IT	DigiGirlz Day	DigiGirlz Day is a one-day event that allows high school girls to explore future career paths in the tech industry.	Held at Microsoft locations in CA, CO, CT, DE, IA, IL, IN, KS, MA, MN, NE, NM, NV, NY, OH, OK, OR, TN, VA, WI, D.C.	Girls only, grades 9–12	www.microsoft.com/en-us/diversity/programs/digigirlz/digigirlzday.aspx	msgirlz@microsoft.com
Journalism	Public Radio Exchange	The Children's Press Line is a youth-led media organization that gives students experience in journalistic research and reporting.	Based in NYC but many local NPR stations host and train youth radio teams	Grades 3–12	www.prx.org/group_accounts/100267-childrens pressline	646–789–4432 817 Broadway, 5th Fl., New York, NY, United States 10003

(Continued)

Chart A.1 (Continued)

Industry Represented	Name	Student-Focused Program	Sites/Locations	Ages Served	Website	Mailing Address of HQ	Phone/Electronic Contact
Journalism	Youth Media Learning Network	Youth Media Learning Network offers professional development and mentoring to young journalists.	YMLN partners with local hosts nationwide to offer its programs	Grades 6–12	www.ymln.org	770 N. Halsted, Ste. 205, Chicago, IL	312–850–2256, Online contact form at website
Law/Legal	Streetlaw	The Corporate Legal Diversity Pipeline program partners corporate legal departments with high schools to increase students' knowledge and interest in the law and legal careers.	Nationwide via local corporate partners.	Grades 9–12	www.streetlaw.org/en/programs/Program/1/Corporate_Legal_Diversity_Pipeline_Program	1010 Wayne Ave, Ste. 870, Silver Spring, MD 20910	301–589–1130, learnmore@streetlaw.org
Math	Association for Women in Mathematics	AWM offers programs, a Mentor Network, and student chapters to encourage girls to pursue careers in math.	Nationwide via chapters	Grades 6–12, college	sites.google.com/site/awmmath/home	11240 Waples Mill Road, Ste. 200, Fairfax, VA 22030	703–934–0163, awm@awm-math.org

Field	Organization	Description	States	Grades	Website	Address	Contact
Math/Engineering	Mathematics, Engineering, Science Achievement (MESA)	MESA offers a STEM-focused academic preparation program for precollege, community college, and university-level students from underserved and minority communities.	AZ, CA, CO, MD, NM, NV, OR, PA, UT, WA	Grades 9–12, college	mesausa.org	See website for links to state-specific MESA chapters	Online contact form at website
Mechanical Engineering	SME Educational Foundation	The PRIME Student Group Mentoring Program pairs mentors with students in PRIME schools to encourage careers in mechanical engineering.	PRIME schools located in: CA, CO, FL, IL, IN, IO, MA, MI, MN, MO, NC, NY, OH, OK, SC, VA, WA, WI	Grades 9–12	www.smeef.org/prime	One SME Drive, P.O. Box 930, Dearborn, MI 48121-0930	313–717–2268, Online contact form at website

(Continued)

Chart A.1 (Continued)

Industry Represented	Name	Student-Focused Program	Sites/Locations	Ages Served	Website	Mailing Address of HQ	Phone/Electronic Contact
Medicine	American Medical Association	AMA's Mentorship Initiative provides mentoring between physicians-in-training and practicing physicians. Doctors Back to School encourages minority students to pursue medical careers.	Nationwide	Grades 6–12	www.ama-assn. org	330 N. Wabash Ave., Chicago, IL 60611–5885	312–464–4335, mas@ama-assn. org
Social Ventures/ Non-profits	Ashoka's Youth Ventures	Ashoka's Dream It Do It Challenge guides and trains young people to launch social ventures.	Nationwide through Youth Venture teams	Grades 6–12	www.youth-venture.org/ dream-it-do-it-challenge	1700 North Moore St., Ste. 2000, Arlington, VA 22209	703–527–8300, yvinfo@ youthventure. org
Software Development	Coder-DOJO	CoderDOJO chapters and events teach kids how to code.	Global, via chapters	Grades K–12	www.coderdojo. com	Find a local dojo through the website	info@coderdojo. com

Software Development	Tech Corps	Tech Corps offers students Web Corps (grades 9–12), Techie Camp (grades 7–8), and Techie Club (grades 3–6).	Based in OH and expanding via chapters to interested schools/sites	Grades 3–12	twenty.techcorps.org	6600 Busch Blvd., Ste. 210, Columbus, OH 43229	614–583–9211, Online contact form at website
STEM	FIRST: For Inspiration and Recognition of Science and Technology	FIRST's programs use team-based robotics to engage kids in STEM fields.	Nationwide, see website to contact local chapters within each program band	Grades K–12	www.firstinspires.org	200 Bedford St., Manchester, NH 03101	603–666–3906
STEM	Project Lead the Way	PLTW develops STEM curricula for elementary, middle, and high schools and provides professional development training for teachers.	Nationwide in partnered schools	Grades K–12	www.pltw.org	3939 Priority Way South Drive, Ste. 400, Indianapolis, IN 46240	877–335–7589, Schoolsupport@pltw.org

Chart A.2 Broad-Based Mentoring

Name	Description of Services	Sites/Locations	Ages Served	Website	Mailing Address	Phone	Electronic Contact
AARP Experience Corps	AARP's Experience Corps members support literacy in the classroom by providing one-on-one or small-group tutoring.	AZ, CA, CT, IL, MA, MD, MI, MN, NY, OH, OR, PA, TX, D.C.	Grades K–5	www.aarp.org/experience-corps	601 E St. NW, Washington, D.C. 20049	888–687–2277	Online contact form at website
Eye to Eye	Eye to Eye pairs kids who have learning disabilities and ADHD with adult mentors who have been similarly labeled as well as offering a NY-based summer camp for kids.	Nationwide via volunteer-run chapters	Grades 6–12	eyetoeyenational.org	150 S. Washington St., Ste. 303, Falls Church, VA 22046	212–537–4429	info@eyetoeyenational.org
Friends of the Children	Friends of the Children provides at-risk kids with a mentor over a 12-year period to help them transition to adulthood.	FL, MA, NY, OR, WA	Grades 6–12	www.friendsofthechildren.org	44 NE Morris St., Portland, OR 97212	503–281–6633	info@friendsofthechildren.org

Organization	Description	Location	Grades	Website	Address	Phone	Email
Girls Inc.	Girls Inc. programs inspire girls to be strong and smart by addressing a variety of issues that challenge young, growing girls.	Nationwide via local nonprofit partners	Grades K–12	girlsinc.org	120 Wall St, New York, NY 10005–3902	212–509–2000	communications@girlsinc.org
Girl Scouts	The Girl Scouts' Fostering a Future (GSFAF) program offers mentors to girls in foster care and the Beyond Bars (GSBB) program offers mentors to girls whose parents are incarcerated.	OR, WA	Grades K–12	GSFAF: www.girlscoutsww.org GSBB: www.girlscoutsw.org	National HQ: 420 Fifth Ave., New York, NY 10018–2798	GSFAF: 800–767–6845 GSBB: 503–977–6815	GSBB: mbaars@girlscoutsosw.org
US Dream Academy	The US Dream Academy provides children at risk of incarceration with academic, social, and values enrichment though mentoring.	FL, IN, MD, PA, TX, UT, D.C.	Grades 3–8	www.usdreamacademy.org	5950 Symphony Woods Rd., Ste. 504 Columbia, MD 21045	800–873–7326	Online contact form at website

Broad-Based Mentoring

Use this section to locate a mentoring opportunity not limited to a specific industry. The organizations listed in this section seek adults who can serve as broad-based role models for youth to help them improve their career and life skills.

Mentoring Focused on Career Prep

This section highlights organizations that focus on helping youth (with special focus on students at risk of dropping out of school) gain specific skills that will prepare them for careers after high school.

Mentoring Focused on College Prep

This section highlights nonprofits/associations that focus on helping low-income youth gain specific academic, psychosocial, and personal skills that will prepare them for entry into college.

Mentoring through Onsite Apprenticeships

This section highlights nonprofits and associations that offer onsite apprenticeships in a variety of fields to low-income youth.

Schools That Use Mentoring

This section highlights public and private school networks that have incorporated career-focused skill building into the traditional K–12 curriculum through a variety of activities such as external internships, adult mentors, and project based and expeditionary learning.

Chart A.3 Mentoring Focused on Career Prep

Name	Description of Services	Sites/ Locations	Ages Served	Website	Mailing Address	Phone	Electronic Contact
4-H National Mentoring Program	Select 4-H chapters offer model programs including: Youth & Families With Promise (UT); Tech Wizards (OR); 4-H LIFE (MO); and the 4-H Tribal Youth National Mentoring Program.	OR, UR, MO (see programs cited) as well as chapters nationwide	Grades 6–12	www.4-h. org/youth-development-programs/mentoring/national-mentoring-program	National HQ: 7100 Connecticut Ave., Chevy Chase, MD 20815	National HQ: 301–961–2800	Visit the website to find a local chapter (http://4-h. org/find/)
Big Brothers/ Big Sisters	BB/BS offers school-based and out-of-school mentoring to support students in becoming healthy, happy, and productive adults.	Nationwide	Grades K–12	www.bbbs.org	National HQ: 2202 N. Westshore Blvd, Ste. 455, Tampa, FL 33607	813–720–8778	Visit the website to search for a local BBBS program
BPSOS	BPSOS' Asian Youth Empowerment Program mentors help Asian American youth achieve academic and career success.	AL, CA, GA, KY, LA, MD, MS, NJ, TX, VA	Grades 9–12	www.bpsos.org	6066 Leesburg Pike, Ste. 100, Falls Church, VA 22041	703–538–2190	info@bpsos. org

(Continued)

Chart A.3 (Continued)

Name	Description of Services	Sites/ Locations	Ages Served	Website	Mailing Address	Phone	Electronic Contact
Campfire USA	Campfire USA's Out-of-School-Time programs include school-based and school break camps, tutoring, mentoring, and club programs to support inner-city, at-risk kids.	Nationwide via selected chapters	Grades K–5	www.campfire. org	1801 Main, Ste. 200, Kansas City, MO, 64108	816–285–2010	Online contact form at website
Concerned Black Men	CBM CARES is a comprehensive outreach project designed to improve academic and life outcomes for African American students.	CA, IN, MA, MD, NJ, PA, TX, VA, D.C.	Grades 6–8	www. cbmnational. org/cbm-cares-national-mentoring-initiative	1313 L Street NW, Ste. 111, Washington, D.C. 20005	888–395–7816	info@ cbmnational. org
Dress for Success	Dress for Success helps low-income women and teen girls successfully transition into the workforce.	Worldwide	Grades 11–12, post high school	www. dressforsuccess. org	National HQ: 32 East 31st St., 7th Fl., New York, NY 10016	212–532–1922	worldwide@ dressforsuccess. org.

Organization	Description	Coverage	Grades	Website	Address	Phone	Email
Goodwill	Goodwill's Good Guides helps teens finish school and transition into productive careers with the guidance of mentors.	CO, GA, IL, NJ, NY, OK, PA, TX	Grades 6–12	www.goodwill.org/goodguides	15810 Indianola Dr., Rockville, MD 20855	800-664-6577	contactus@goodwill.org
Jobs Corps	Job Corps offers education, training, and adult mentors to help students earn a high school diploma or GED and find a good job.	Nationwide	Grades 9–12, post high school	www.jobcorps.gov	300 New Jersey Ave NW, Ste. 900, Washington, D.C. 20001	202-693-3000	national_office@jobcorps.gov
Jobs for America's Graduates	JAG offers school-to-work transition programs focused on helping at-risk youth graduate and get into a career.	Nationwide	Grades 6–12, post high school	www.jag.org	1729 King St., Ste. 100, Alexandria, VA 22314	703-684-9479	Online contact form at website
National Coalition of 100 Black Women	The NCBW's LEAD Mentoring Program offers guidance to African American girls to prepare them for a full life and career.	Nationwide via selected chapters	Grades 6–12	www.ncbw.org	1925 Adam C. Powell Jr. Blvd., Ste. 1L, New York, NY 10026	212-222-5660	adminassist@nc100bw.org
The National Guard Youth Foundation	NGYF's Youth ChalleNGe Program provides high school dropouts with the opportunity to improve their life skills, education, and employability.	Nationwide plus Puerto Rico	Grades 9–12	www.ngyf.org	415 N Lee St., Alexandria, VA 22314	703-684-5437	info@ngyf.org

Chart A.4 Mentoring Focused on College Prep

Name	Description of Services	Sites/Locations	Ages Served	Website	Mailing Address	Phone	Electronic Contact
"I Have A Dream" Foundation	The "I Have A Dream" Foundation provides low-income children with a long-term program of academic support, mentoring, tutoring, and tuition assistance.	CA, CO, FL, IA, ID, NJ, NV, NY, OR, VA, WI, D.C.	Grades 6–12	www.ihaveadream foundation.org	330 Seventh Ave., 20th Fl., New York, NY 10001	212–293–5480	info@ihaveadream foundation.org
100 Black Men of America, Inc.	100 Black Men of America's Mentoring the 100 Way provides African American boys with mentors to help prepare them for college/careers and life.	Nationwide via chapters	Grades 3–12	100blackmen.org/mentoring.aspx	141 Auburn Ave., Atlanta, GA 30303	404–688–5100	info@100blackmen.org
College Success Foundation	CSF's programs provide mentors to low-income students with mentors to help them prepare for college.	WA (state), D.C.	Grades 6–12, post high school	www.collegesuccess foundation.org	1605 NW Sammamish Rd., Ste. 200, Issaquah, WA 98027	877–655–4097	info@collegesuccess foundation.org

Organization	Description	Location	Grades	Website	Address	Phone	Email
Digital Network Community Development Corporation	DNCD.C.'s Kinetic Potential Scholars program provides long-term mentorship to at-risk students.	Based in D.C. but plans to expand to CA, FL, GA, IL, MA, NJ, NV, NY, OH, PA, TX	Grades 9–12, post high school	www.digitalnetworkgroup.net/power.php	Prince George County Maryland, 1100 Mercantile Ln., Ste. 115A, Largo, MD 20774	301–883–8255	innovation@digitalnetworkgroup.net
Step Up	Step Up offers programs that empower disadvantaged, minority girls to become college bound and career ready.	CA, IL, NY	Grades 9–12	www.suwn.org	510 South Hewitt Ste. #111, Los Angeles, CA 90013	213–382–9161	national@suwn.org
Boys Hope/Girls Hope	BHGH's College Road program prepares academically motivated, low-income youth for college.	AZ, CA, CO, IL, KS, LA, MD, MI, MO, NY, OH, PA	Grades 9–12	www.boyshopegirlshope.org	12120 Bridgeton Square Dr., Bridgeton, MO 63044	314–298–1250	hope@bhgh.org

Chart A.5 Mentoring Through Onsite Apprenticeships

Name	Description of Services	Sites/Locations	Ages Served	Website	Mailing Address	Phone	Electronic Contact
Spark	Spark provides one-on-one, mentored, workplace apprenticeships to disadvantaged youth.	CA, IL, PA	Grades 6–8	www.sparkprogram.org	555 De Haro St., San Francisco, CA 94107	213–344–4848	Online contact form at website
StreetWise Partners	Through SWP's Career Ventures, disadvantaged, low-income students intern for three months in a corporate setting under the guidance of a mentor.	NY, D.C.	Post high school	www.streetwisepartners.org	65 Broadway, 19th Fl., New York, NY 10006	646–705–0029	info@streetwisepartners.org
Year Up	Year Up is a one-year, intensive training program that provides low-income, young adults with a combination of hands-on skill development, college credits, and corporate internships.	CA, FL, GA, IL, MA, MD, NY, PA, RI, WA, D.C.	Post high school	www.yearup.org	45 Milk St., 9th Fl., Boston, MA 02109	855–932–7871	volunteer@yearup.org

Chart A.6 Schools That Use Mentoring

Name	Description of School or Program	Sites/Locations	Ages Served	Website	Mailing Address	Phone	Electronic Contact
Big Picture Learning	BPL's Learning Through Internship/Interest pairs students with adult mentors (an expert in the field of the student's interest) and has the duo work on projects together.	CA, CO, CN, DE, IN, MI, NJ, NY, OK, PA, RI, TN, VT, WA	Grades K–12	www.bigpicture.org	325 Public St., Providence, RI 02905	401–752–3442	info@bigpicture learning.org
California Partnerships Academy	CPA's career academies offer small-group learning programs in existing high school that integrate academics, career technical education, business partnerships, mentoring, and internships.	450+ school sizes across California	Grades 10–12	www.cde.ca.gov/ci/gs/hs/cpagen.asp	1430 N St., Sacramento, CA 95814	916–319–0800	jwinthrop@cde.ca.gov

(Continued)

Chart A.6 (Continued)

Name	Description of School or Program	Sites/Locations	Ages Served	Website	Mailing Address	Phone	Electronic Contact
Christo Rey Schools	Christo Rey students intern with professional corporate partners to gain work experience and to develop skills.	AZ, CA, CO, GA, IL, IN, KS, LA, MA, MD, MI, MN, NC, NJ, NY, NV, OH, OK, OR, PA, TN, TX, WA, WI, D.C.	Grades 6–8	www.cristorey network.org	14 East Jackson Blvd., Ste. 1200, Chicago, IL 60604	312–784–7200	Visit the website to access a school directory
Citizen Schools	CS's all-volunteer Citizen Teachers help students make connections between school, college, and careers.	CA, IL, MA, NC, NJ, NY, TX	Grades 6–8	www. citizenschools.org	308 Congress St., 5th Fl., Boston, WA 02210	617–695–2300	Online contact form at website
Communities in Schools	CIS identifies and mobilizes local resources, including mentors, to provide a range of services to kids at risk of dropping out of school.	AK, CA, DE, FL, GA, IA, IL, IN, IO, KS, LA, MA, MI, NC, NE, NM, NV, OH, OK, PA, SC, TN, TX, VA, WV, D.C.	Grades 3–12	www. communities inschools.org	2345 Crystal Dr., Ste. 700, Arlington, VA 22202	800–247–4543	info@cisnet.org

Organization	Description	States	Grades	Website	Address	Phone	Email
ConnectEd	CE's work-based learning uses internships and adult mentors to prepare students for careers.	CA	Grades 9–12	www.connecteD.california.org	2150 Shattuck, Ste. 1200, Berkeley, CA 94704	510–849–4945	Info@ConnectED.California.org
EdVisions	As part of the EdVisions curriculum, high school students complete project based learning using adult mentors.	CA, HI, KA, MN, NJ, NV, PA, WA, WI	Grades 9–12	www.edvisions.com	501 Main St, PO Box 601, Henderson, MN 56044	507–248–3738	keven@edvisionsschools.org
Envision Education	Through the Workplace Learning Experience, high school students intern at partner organizations where they learn from an employer mentor and complete a project with measureable outcomes.	CA (primarily) but partner schools are also in HI, MA, and WA	Grades 9–12	www.envisionschools.org	111 Myrtle St., Ste. 203, Oakland, CA 94607	510–451–2415	info@envisionschools.org

(Continued)

Chart A.6 (Continued)

Name	Description of School or Program	Sites/Locations	Ages Served	Website	Mailing Address	Phone	Electronic Contact
Expeditionary Learning Schools	The Expeditionary Learning model prepares students for success in college, career, and citizenship.	AZ, CA, CO, CT, DE, FL, GA, IA, ID, IL, IN, KS, MA, MD, ME, MI, MN, MO, NC, NM, NY, OH, OR, PA, RI, SC, TN, TX, UT, WA, WI, WV	Grades K–12	elschools.org/	247 West 35th St., 8th Fl, New York, NY 10001	212–239–4455	info@elschools.org
International Network for Public Schools	INPS's Career and Technical Education and career academy high schools prepare students for specific careers through mentors and internships.	CA, MD, NY, VA, D.C.	Grades K–12	internationalsnps.org	50 Broadway, Ste. 2200, New York, NY 10004	212–868–5180	info@internationalsnps.org

Mentor Foundation USA	The Mentoring in Schools program matches low-income students with professionals from the business community and the Authentic Career Experiences program offers experiential learning for older students at partner companies.	D.C.	Grades 9–12	www.mentor foundationusa.org	2900 K Street, N.W. #501, Washington, D.C. 20007	202–536–1592	usa@mentor foundation.org

(Continued)

Chart A.6 (Continued)

Name	Description of School or Program	Sites/Locations	Ages Served	Website	Mailing Address	Phone	Electronic Contact
National Academies Foundation	NAF's career academies are organized around one of five career themes, and students take industry-specific classes (in addition to standard college prep curriculum), plus they participate in field trips, internships, mentoring, and job coaching.	AL, AZ, CA, CO, CT, DE, FL, GA, HI, ID, IL, IN, KS, KY, LA, MA, MD, MN, MO, MS, NC, NE, NH, NJ, NM, NV, NY, OK, PA, RI, SC, SD, TX, UT, VA, WA, WI, D.C.	Grades 11–12	naf.org, includes a list of the five career themes the NAF focuses on	218 W. 40th St, 5th Fl., New York, NY 10018	212–635–2400	Online contact form at website
New Tech Network	NTN works with partners to provide an instructional approach centered on project based learning and integrated technology	AK, AZ, CA, CO, CT, DE, FL, GA, ID, IL, IN, IO, KY, LA, MA, MI, MO, NC, NM, NY, OH, OK, SC, SD, TN, TX, VA, WA, WV, D.C.	Grades 9–12	www. newtechnetwork. org	1250 Main St., Ste. 100, Napa, CA 94559	707–253–6951	inquiry@ newtechnetwork. org

Chart A.7 Online Clearinghouses

Organizational Name	Website	Brief Description
Achieve	achieve.org	Offers research, advocacy, and technical assistance to help states promote college/career readiness
America's Promise	www.americaspromise.org	Offers a searchable database by zip code
California Mentoring Partnership	www.camentoring partnership.org	Contact CMP to enter into its mentor database and be connected to opportunities
Center for Education and Workforce	www.uschamberfoundation.org/center-education-and-workforce	Offers research, advocacy, and national conference to promote best practices in K–12 education
Change the Equation	changetheequation.org	Offers the STEMworks database to highlight kid-focused STEM learning programs across the nation
Connectory	www.theconnectory.org	Offers a database of hands-on STEM learning opportunities for elementary to high school–aged youth.
Connecticut Mentoring Partnership	www.preventionworksct.org/what/mentoring/about	Sign up to become a mentor at this website for mentoring opportunities in Connecticut
Delaware Mentoring Council	www.delawarementoring.org	Offers a searchable database by zip code
Encore	www.encore.org	Assists older adults in finding a second career in charity work / civil service
Friends for Youth—Bay Area Mentoring	www.bayareamentoring.org	Lists mentoring/other volunteer opportunities in the San Francisco Bay (CA) Area
Grads of Life	gradsoflife.org/connect-share	Offers searchable database by zip code

(Continued)

Chart A.7 (Continued)

Organizational Name	Website	Brief Description
Grantmakers for Education	www.edfunders.org	Offers a variety of resources for education philanthropy
HandsOn Network	www.handsonnetwork. org	Partners with local and national organizations to organize large projects and attract/recruit volunteers for single day service events
Idealist	www.idealist.org	Offers a database of nonprofits, volunteer opportunities, and nonprofit jobs searchable by city/state
Illinois Mentoring Partnership	www.ilmentoring.org	Offers a searchable database by zip code
Indiana Mentoring Partnership	www.abetterhour.org	Offers a searchable database by zip code
Iowa Mentoring Partnership	www.iowamentoring. org	Offers a searchable database by zip code
Kansas Mentors	kansasmentors.org	Offers a searchable database by zip code
MASS Mentoring Partnership	www.massmentors.org	Offers a searchable database by zip code
MENTOR: National Mentoring Partnership	www.mentoring.org	Offers a searchable database by zip code
Mentor Colorado	www.comentoring.org	Offers searchable database by zip code
Mentor Michigan	www.michigan.gov/ mentormichigan	Offers a searchable database by zip code
MentorNet.org	mentornet.org	Connects college-based STEM students with professionals in a variety of STEM fields for training, advice, and guidance during a four-month mentoring cycle.

Organizational Name	Website	Brief Description
Mentor New York	www.mentornewyork. org	Offers a searchable database by zip code
Mentoring Partnership of North Carolina	www.ncmentoring.org	Offers a searchable database by zip code
Midlands Mentoring Partnership	mmpomaha.org	Offers a searchable database by zip code
Million Women Mentors	www. millionwomenmentors. org	A national initiative that began in 2014 to support the engagement of (STEM) mentors for girls and young women
National Girls Collaborative Project	ngcproject.org/about-ngcp	A national initiative to bring together organizations committed to informing and encouraging girls to pursue careers in science, technology, engineering, and mathematics (STEM)
Newark Mentoring Movement	www. newarkmentoring.org	Offers a list of Newark-based organizations seeking mentors
Points of Light Foundation	www.pointsoflight.org	Offers a list of volunteer opportunities and nonprofits that can be searched using specific terms
ReServe	reserveinc.org/about	Matches volunteers 55 and older with nonprofits
Rhode Island Mentoring Partnership	mentorri.org	Offers a searchable database by zip code
Senior Corps of Retired Executives (SCORE)	www.score.org	Offers a searchable database by zip code
Stem Connector	www.stemconnector. org	Offers a searchable nationwide STEM directory

(*Continued*)

Organizational Name	Website	Brief Description
Taproot Foundation	www.taprootfoundation.org	Offers search capability for available projects by zip code and the ability to generate a list of consultants working in specialized areas
The Mentoring Center of Central Ohio	www.mentoringcenterco.org	Sign up to become a mentor at this website for central Ohio mentor opportunities
The Mentoring Partnership of Minnesota	www.mpmn.org/Home.aspx	Offers a searchable database by zip code
The Mentoring Partnership of New York	www.mentoring.org/newyork	Offers a searchable database by zip code
The Mentoring Partnership and Resource Center	www.partnersinmentoring.org	Offers a searchable database by zip code for Southeastern PA
Vermont's Mentoring Partnership	www.mobiusmentors.org	Offers a list of opportunities and nonprofit agencies by county
Virginia Mentoring Partnership	www.vamentoring.org	Offers a searchable database by zip code
Volunteer Florida	www.flamentorpartnership.org	Offers a searchable database by zip code
Volunteer Match	www.volunteermatch.org	Customizable search by state
Mentoring Works Washington	www.mentoringworkswa.org	Offers a searchable database by zip code
National Mentoring Resource Center	www.nationalmentoringresourcecenter.org	Serves as a comprehensive and reliable resource for mentoring tools and information, program and training materials, and technical assistance

Online Clearinghouses

Use this section to find web-based clearinghouses that list thousands of volunteer opportunities with hundreds of organizations. Because these clearinghouses typically work at the state, city, or county level, they can provide a variety of volunteer opportunities within your immediate community, including mentoring for teens and young adults.

Career and Technology Education (CTE) Resources

Career and technology education is a term applied to schools, institutions, and educational programs that prepare youth and young adults for a wide range of careers in the skilled trades, applied sciences, and modern technologies. CTE programs offer both academic and career-oriented courses, and many provide

Chart A.8 Career and Technology Education (CTE) Resources

Organizational Name	Mission	Web Address	Address	Phone
Association for Career and Technical Education	Dedicated to the advancement of CTE and to providing resources to CTE programs nationwide	www. acteonline. org	410 King St., Alexandria, VA 22314	800–826–9972
Advance CTE	Advance CTE is an advocate for policies and legislation that enhance and sustain high-quality CTE programs throughout the nation	www. careertech. org	8484 Georgia Ave., Ste. 320, Silver Spring, MD 20910	301–588–9630

Chart A.9 Community Colleges

Source	Website	Brief Description
Washington Monthly's College Guide Rankings	www.washingtonmonthly.com	Top 50 colleges ranked by eight categories
The Best Schools	www.thebestschools.org	Top 50 colleges ranked by five categories
The Aspen Institute's Prize for Community College Excellence	www.aspeninstitute.org/policy-work/college-excellence/overview	A list of the top 120 community colleges based on three categories and organized by state
College Measures.org's two-year College Tool	www.collegemeasures.org/2-year_colleges/home/	Offers customizable search using data such as "success rate"
College Navigator	nces.ed.gov/collegenavigator/	Offers highly customizable searches of a nationwide database
US News & World Report College Rankings and Reviews	colleges.usnews.rankingsandreviews.com/best-colleges	Basic, searchable stats on specific two- and four-year colleges and listings for all "regional colleges"
American Association of Community Colleges	www.aacc.nche.edu	Offers a community college finder
National Collegiate Honors Council	nchchonors.org/members-area/member-institutions-4/	Offers a list of two- and four-year colleges with honors programs

students with the opportunity to gain work experience through internships, job shadowing, on-the-job training, and industry-certification opportunities.

Community Colleges

The American Association of Community Colleges (www.aacc.nche.edu) represents nearly twelve hundred community colleges and more than thirteen million students. Community college programs have long offered students specialized learning thanks to strong industry partnerships. The AACC's website offers a dynamic listing of current programs nationwide, from aerospace to green job training to the nuclear industry (see www.aacc. nche.edu/ABOUTCC/Pages/college-industry_partnership.aspx).

The list below offers additional third-party sources for researching the programs and strengths of community colleges nationwide.

Sources for Mentor Training and Skill Building

The following sources are provided as additional tools for developing skills in mentoring teens and young adults.

- **www.mentor.org**: Based in Oakland, CA, this organization offers training and technical assistance to groups that work with adult mentors.
- **www.gallupstrengthscenter.com**: This website offers strengths coaching kits and comprehensive coaching materials to mentors.
- **Two Minute Mentor: The Only Life Advice You'll Ever Need**: available as a Kindle download at Amazon, this book by Tim Hoch uses life stories and advice to help readers navigate everyday problems.

Author's Note

In 2010, I was diagnosed with cancer. I faced an inevitable possibility that my life could be shortened. The good news is: it seems I have surpassed this crisis. I am certain I changed as a result.

As with many survivors, I gained a new perspective from this experience. It's forced me to ask, "What have I done in my life that is important, and should be carried on?"

I have concluded that success is not about accumulation, possessions, or position, but about the individual people whose lives we've touched. Can we help them be better? What role do we have to contribute?

And how?

If, after reading *Teach to Work*, you are considering a mentoring role to share your life experience, your choices, and your pathway with a student who is lost or misdirected, then I will have done my job.

Index

About the Author

Patty Alper is president of the Alper Portfolio Group, a marketing and consulting company, and is a board member of both the Network for Teaching Entrepreneurship (NFTE) and US2020, the White House initiative to build mentorship in STEM (science, technology, engineering, and math) careers. She has also been appointed to the corporate committee for Million Women Mentors. Through her services on the national board of NFTE, Patty's vision served as the groundwork for the Adopt-a-Class program she founded in 2001. During her years of service at NFTE, she invited countless business leaders to join her in a mentoring capacity, helping teachers across the country inspire and coach entrepreneurship students on their business plans. Prior to joining NFTE, Patty spent five years working with incarcerated, runaway, and suicidal youth in Iowa's Youth Detention System, and she served as a counselor to psychotic adolescents at Chestnut Lodge, a long-term psychiatric hospital in Maryland.